Sunset
Bulbs
FOR ALL SEASONS

By the Editors of Sunset Books and Sunset Magazine

*Yellow daffodils and blue Dutch irises keep company
with colorful annuals and perennials.*

Sunset Publishing Corporation • Menlo Park, California

GLOBES of Allium sphaerocephalum *rise above spikes of purple* Salvia.

A PALETTE OF SEASONAL COLOR...

Bulbs offer an easy and delightful way to add striking accents of color to your garden, whether you plant sweeping displays with a lavish hand or confine your efforts to a few containers of seasonal blooms.

Though many favorites bloom in spring, you'll find a number of bulbs here—identified by both botanical and common names—that flower in other seasons. Entries in our Catalog of Favorite Bulbs offer information on each bulb, so you can evaluate its suitability for your climate and garden conditions.

After you've selected the bulbs you want for your garden, you'll learn the best way to plant and care for them to ensure success: a spectacular array of glorious blooms.

For carefully checking our manuscript, special thanks go to James Bauml, Los Angeles State and County Arboretum, Arcadia, California; Victoria Jahn, Brooklyn Botanic Garden, New York; Wayne Roderick, director emeritus, Regional Parks Botanic Garden, Berkeley, California; and Julius Wadekamper, bulb nurseryman, Elk River, Minnesota. We also thank M. Nevin Smith, Wintergreen Nursery; Roger Reynolds Nursery; and Lew Whitney, Roger's Gardens, for their assistance with photography; and Rebecca La Brum for her thorough editing.

Research & Text
Philip Edinger

Coordinating Editor
Cornelia Fogle

Design
Roger Flanagan

Illustrations
Ginny Mickelson

Photo Editor
JoAnn Masaoka

PHOTOGRAPHERS

Davids & Royston Bulb Co.: 67 (center right). **Derek Fell:** 6, 9 (top right), 10, 15 (right), 22 (bottom center, bottom right), 27 (bottom right), 30 (bottom center), 35 (bottom left), 38 (top right), 43 (top left), 46 (bottom center, bottom right), 51 (bottom right), 67 (top right), 70 (center, center right). **Gerald Fredrick:** 67 (top left), 75 (center left). **Harry Haralambou:** 9 (bottom). **Pamela Harper:** 14, 27 (bottom left), 30 (bottom right), 35 (top center, top right), 38 (bottom center), 43 (top center), 51 (top right), 59 (top center), 67 (top center), 70 (bottom center), 75 (top left, top center). **Saxon Holt:** 3 (center), 19. **Horticultural Photography:** 2, 27 (top right), 35 (top left, bottom right), 38 (bottom right), 43 (bottom left), 46 (top right), 62 (bottom right). **Ells Marugg:** 11 (bottom), 13 (right), 22 (top left, bottom left), 27 (top center), 30 (top left), 38 (top left, bottom left), 43 (top right), 46 (left), 54 (bottom left), 67 (bottom right), 70 (bottom left). **Jack McDowell:** 51 (top left). **Norm Plate:** 3 (left), 4, 22 (top right), 62 (top left), 70 (center left). **Bill Ross:** 15 (left), 16, 27 (top left), 54 (top center, bottom right), 59 (bottom right), 62 (top right, bottom left), 70 (bottom right), 75 (top right). **David Stubbs:** 13 (left), 75 (bottom left). **Michael Thompson:** 51 (bottom left). **Darrow Watt:** 9 (top left), 11 (top), 30 (top right, bottom left), 51 (top center), 59 (top right, bottom left), 75 (center, center right). **Rod Whitlow:** 7 (top). **Russ Widstrand:** 1. **Tom Wyatt:** 3 (right), 54 (top left), 62 (bottom center), 67 (bottom left), 70 (top), 78.

Cover: Assembly of early-blooming bulbs includes daffodils in yellow, yellow with cream; lilac freesias; and a scattering of white narcissus. Photography by Tom Wyatt. Cover design by JoAnn Masaoka.

Editorial Director, Sunset Books: Kenneth Winchester

Eighth printing April 1995

CONTENTS

THE SPLENDOR OF BULBS

Almost everyone is at some time touched by the beauty of bulbs. The experience may be an overpowering one or a more simple, personal pleasure—the impact of massed color and bloom at a public planting of tulips, the delicacy and detail of a single potted daffodil. Sometimes the encounter with bulbs is totally unexpected—finding a blooming snowdrop or crocus where only bare snow had been the previous day. And at other times, we expect to see their flowers. What is a June wedding without arrangements of gladiolus and a spray or two of lily-of-the-valley in the bridal bouquet?

One has only to think of a few popular bulbs—daffodil, tulip, iris, hyacinth, and gladiolus, for example—to realize that there's considerable difference in appearance among the plants we casually refer to as bulbs. In fact, bulbs are so varied that some may go unrecognized as such: gloxinias, dahlias, and ranunculus, to name just a few.

These examples bring up an obvious question: What is the common thread that draws these apparently unrelated plants together?

The answer lies buried beneath the soil. All the plants referred to as "bulbs" grow from structures that function as storage organs, as depots where the plants accumulate nutrients that provide the energy for growth and bloom in the year to come. Botanists draw a hard and fast line between true bulbs and other structures with a similar function, but generations of gardeners have used "bulb" as a generic term for plants that grow from bulb*like* organs: corms, tubers, rhizomes, and tuberous roots (see pages 80 and 81).

Though these "other bulbs" differ in actual structure from true bulbs, all function in basically the same fashion, bringing forth each year, from unglamorous packages, their varied and beautiful blossoms.

CAN SPRING be far away? Narcissus *'February Gold' gives early signal beneath European white birches.*

A WORLD OF BULBS

An overwhelming number of bulbs are native to a broad latitudinal strip extending from Spain and North Africa through the Mediterranean region, eastward through the Near East, Turkey, and Iran, and on as far as western China. Actual summer and winter temperatures vary considerably in this vast territory, but nearly all parts of the area experience winter precipitation (rain or snow) and a hot, dry summer. The same climatic conditions prevail in California, parts of Chile, and South Africa; these regions, too, are homeland to a number of popular bulbs.

The bulblike structure evolved as an adaptation to the annual alternation of wet and dry periods. Growth takes place during the cooler, moister months (autumn, winter, part of spring). As days lengthen and grow warmer, flowers start to appear, sometimes seeming to rush into bloom while conditions are still favorable for setting seed. Then, as flowers fade and seeds mature, the bulb accumulates a supply of nutrients that will keep it alive (in a dormant state) after summer heat and dryness have withered foliage and put an end to the annual growing period.

A lesser, but still significant, number of bulbs, most notably summer-flowering African types such as *Gloriosa* and *Zantedeschia*, also come from regions that have a wet/dry alternation. But here, rainy weather comes during the hot summer months, while winters are cool and dry. Plants grow during the rainy season, then go dormant (or grow more slowly) when cool, dry conditions resume.

A few bulbs, such as *Zephyranthes* and *Habranthus*, are native to areas where moist and dry spells alternate irregularly. These types may flower more than once during a year, whenever they receive enough rainfall to stimulate another growth cycle.

Of course, not all bulbous plants fit into this neat geographical pattern. *Crinum* and *Colocasia,* for example, grow in regions of year-round humidity, where development of a bulblike structure in response to climatic extremes would seem to be unnecessary. In general, these plants belong to families richly represented in the world's principal bulb regions, but they grow on the outskirts of the usual ranges.

A long history

An appreciation of bulbs is nothing new. Cretan frescoes and vases dating from about 1600 B.C. are decorated with unmistakable iris and lily motifs; both art and written records attest that the early Egyptians grew various bulbs for ornament and ceremonial purposes, among them anemones, irises, lilies, and narcissus.

The Greeks, too, were familiar with the beauty of bulbs. The writings of the philosopher/botanist Theophrastus (around 340 B.C.) mention plants we know today as allium, anemone, crocus, cyclamen, gladiolus, grape hyacinth, lily, narcissus, ranunculus, and scilla. Roman records and poetry mention the use of various bulbs in religious rites and extol the beauties of particular bulb flowers. And Biblical references to bulbs abound in both the Old and New Testaments.

Items of commerce. The Minoans of Crete were perhaps the first to realize any profit from bulbs, or at least the first to recognize their barter potential. Presumably, they originated the saffron trade, marketing the dried stigmas of *Crocus sativus* for use as a sort of drug. Saffron is still produced and sold today, fetching very high prices as a cooking spice.

Tulipomania. The saffron trade pales, however, in comparison to history's first recorded horticultural craze: the "tulipomania" of the early 17th century. The story of tulipomania really begins in 1554, when a Belgian named Ogier de Busbecq was sent to Constantinople as Austrian envoy to the court of Sultan Suleiman I, then ruler of the Ottoman Empire. During his stay, de Busbecq encountered a flower

RIOTOUS springtime display features tulips in variety backed up by Narcissus *in yellow and white.*

totally unknown to him: the tulip, which had been cultivated in Turkey for some time.

When he returned from Turkey to Vienna, de Busbecq brought tulip bulbs with him, some of which were acquired by the botanist Carolus Clusius (Charles L'Ecluse). Clusius became so fond of tulips that, when he moved to the Netherlands in 1593 to work at the botanical gardens in Leyden, he took bulbs with him. Their striking flowers naturally attracted interest, but Clusius jealously guarded his tulip collection, asking impossibly high prices for the precious plants. Of course, this exclusive ownership couldn't last forever; it wasn't long before a number of bulbs were stolen straight out of his garden. Clusius's loss was the gain of wealthy Dutch burghers, among whom possession of rare tulips became the ultimate status symbol.

As the prestige of tulips increased, so did their prices. Stock-market-like speculation and trading marked the exchange of bulbs, which reached its frenzied zenith in the years 1634 to 1637.

Inevitably, the tulip market "crashed"; countless investors who had bought without the assets to back up their purchases were instantly bankrupted.

Though tulipomania was a catastrophe for unlucky investors at the time, it had far-reaching positive benefits. First, it made the enterprising Netherlanders aware of the potential value of bulb production, laying the first stone in the foundation of today's thriving Dutch bulb industry. The tulip craze also had a noticeable effect on 17th-century art: the beautiful blossoms are frequently featured in the masterworks of the Dutch and Flemish floral painters.

Bulbs then, now & tomorrow

The tulip's introduction to Europe, and the fad popularity it enjoyed, signaled more than just an exaggerated interest in an exotic flower. The 17th century saw the beginning of increased contact with and acquisition of horticultural exotics, largely through the activities of proliferating ranks of botanist/explorers and the East India companies of The Netherlands and England. From the abrupt end of tulipomania until 1800, a wealth of plants found their way to European botanical gardens and to the private estates of wealthy landholders.

This "domestication" of exotic flowers established interest in particular plants—tulips and hyacinths, among bulbs—and consequently led, in the 19th century, to the foundation of great commercial nurseries. (The Dutch bulb specialist firm Van Tubergen, established in the early 1800s, is still a thriving part of the now international bulb business.) These establishments both furthered the development of many specialty plants and made them available to a growing class of individuals with time and money to spend on gardening.

The period from the late 19th century up to the present could well be called the Age of Specialists. During this time, nurseries and individual growers have taken special interest in particular bulbs, and through

CASCADING over windowbox as well as standing upright, tuberous begonias provide continuous summer color.

dedicated hybridizing have brought daffodils, dahlias, gladiolus, irises, and tulips (among others) to their current state of glorious refinement. This interest has given rise to a separate class of bulb grower: the absolute specialist, who markets only one type of bulb. Extreme specialization has in no way diminished the general bulb trade, though; specialist and generalist alike have benefited from an ever-increasing demand by a bulb-conscious gardening public.

Despite plant breeders' stunning achievements with particular bulbs, there's still room for further development, among both "developed" bulbs and those that have yet to be extensively hybridized. Moreover, a resurgence of plant-collecting activity has sent botanists back into Greece, Turkey, and other areas not explored since the 19th century. Other expeditions are traveling into the rugged hills and mountains of Iran and the southern Soviet Union, parts of the "bulb motherland" where exploration had been severely limited by hostilities and inadequate transportation.

As a result of recent exploration, newly discovered species are slowly entering cultivation—species that may themselves come to enrich our gardens, or that may provide parent material for undreamed-of future hybrids.

SPRING BLOOM SEASON

Botanical names / Common names	Pink	Red	Orange	Yellow	Cream	White	Blue	Lavender	Purple	Multicolor	Fragrant	Shade	Container
Allium / Drumsticks, golden garlic, star of Persia	■	■		■		■	■	■	■		■		
Alstroemeria / Peruvian lily	■	■	■	■	■	■		■					■
Anemone / Windflower	■	■				■	■		■				■
Babiana / Baboon flower		■			■	■	■	■	■				■
Bletilla striata / Chinese ground orchid						■		■				■	
Brodiaea / Ithuriel's spear				■		■	■	■	■				■
Calochortus / Fairy lantern, globe tulip, Mariposa lily	■	■		■	■	■		■	■	■			■
Camassia / Camass					■	■	■						
Chionodoxa / Glory-of-the-snow	■					■	■						
Clivia miniata / Kaffir lily		■	■	■								■	■
Colchicum luteum / Meadow saffron				■									■
Convallaria majalis / Lily-of-the-valley	■					■					■	■	■
Crinum	■					■					■		
Crocus				■	■	■	■	■	■	■			■
Cyclamen	■	■				■		■	■			■	■
Dietes / Fortnight lily, African iris				■		■							■
Endymion / Bluebell	■					■	■				■	■	■
Eranthis hyemalis / Winter aconite				■									
Eremurus / Foxtail lily	■		■	■	■	■							
Erythronium / Adder's tongue, dog-tooth violet	■					■		■	■			■	
Freesia	■	■	■	■	■	■	■	■	■		■		■
Fritillaria / Fritillary		■	■	■	■	■			■			■	
Galanthus / Snowdrop						■							
Gladiolus	■	■	■	■	■	■		■	■	■			
Haemanthus katharinae / Blood lily	■	■										■	■
Hemerocallis / Daylily	■	■	■	■	■			■	■	■	■		■
Hippeastrum / Amaryllis	■	■	■			■				■			
Hyacinthus / Hyacinth	■	■		■	■	■	■		■		■		■
Ipheion uniflorum / Spring star flower						■	■						■
Iris	■	■	■	■	■	■	■	■	■	■	■		■
Ixia / African corn lily	■	■	■	■	■	■							■

PERUVIAN LILIES (Alstroemeria) *grace the garden in late spring, presenting an increasingly lavish display each year.*

HARBINGERS OF SPRING, snowdrops (Galanthus nivalis) brave the snow to announce the season.

FESTIVE Dutch hybrid crocuses are a traditional component of early spring bulb display.

9

Botanical names / Common names	Pink	Red	Orange	Yellow	Cream	White	Blue	Lavender	Purple	Multicolor	Fragrant	Shade	Container
Lachenalia / Cape cowslip	■	■	■	■									■
Lapeirousia		■				■							■
Leucocoryne ixioides / Glory-of-the-sun							■				■		■
Leucojum / Snowflake	■					■						■	■
Lilium / Lily	■	■	■	■	■	■		■	■	■	■		■
Muscari / Grape hyacinth						■	■	■			■		■
Narcissus / Daffodil, jonquil				■	■	■				■	■		■
Ornithogalum / Chincherinchee, star of Bethlehem						■					■		■
Oxalis	■	■		■		■		■					■
Puschkinia scilloides						■	■						■
Ranunculus asiaticus	■	■	■	■	■	■				■			■
Scilla / Squill	■					■	■		■			■	■
Sparaxis / Harlequin flower	■	■	■	■		■			■	■			■
Tritonia / Flame freesia	■	■	■	■		■							■
Tulbaghia								■					■
Tulipa / Tulip	■	■	■	■	■	■		■	■	■			■
Veltheimia viridifolia	■											■	■
Watsonia	■	■	■			■		■			■		■
Zantedeschia / Calla, calla lily	■	■	■	■	■	■		■	■			■	■
Zephyranthes / Zephyr flower, fairy lily	■			■		■							■

MASSES OF DAYLILIES (Hemerocallis) *light up the late spring scene; they'll keep blooming into early summer.*

CONGENIAL COMPANIONS Freesia
and Spanish bluebell (Endymion) *share
bloom time and cultural needs.*

*OFFERING almost every color but blue,
cheerful ranunculus brighten the springtime
scene with their fluffy blooms.*

SUMMER BLOOM SEASON

Botanical names / Common names	Pink	Red	Orange	Yellow	Cream	White	Blue	Lavender	Purple	Multicolor	Fragrant	Shade	Container
Achimenes	■						■	■	■			■	■
Agapanthus / Lily-of-the-Nile							■	■					■
Allium / Drumsticks, golden garlic, star of Persia	■	■		■		■	■	■	■		■		
Alstroemeria / Peruvian lily	■	■	■	■	■	■		■					■
Amaryllis belladonna / Belladonna lily, naked lady	■										■		
Begonia tuberhybrida / Tuberous begonia	■	■	■	■	■	■				■		■	■
Belamcanda chinensis / Blackberry lily			■										
Brodiaea / Ithuriel's spear				■		■	■	■	■				■
Caladium hortulanum / Fancy-leafed caladium										■		■	■
Calochortus / Fairy lantern, globe tulip, Mariposa lily	■	■		■	■	■		■	■	■			■
Canna	■	■	■	■	■	■					■		■
Colchicum / Meadow saffron	■					■		■	■				■
Crinum	■					■					■		■
Crocosmia / Montbretia		■	■	■									
Cyclamen	■	■				■		■	■			■	■
Dahlia	■	■	■	■	■	■		■	■	■			■
Dietes / Fortnight lily, African iris				■		■							■
Eucomis / Pineapple flower											■	■	■
Galtonia candicans / Summer hyacinth						■					■		■
Gladiolus	■	■	■	■	■	■		■	■	■			■
Gloriosa rothschildiana / Glory lily, climbing lily										■			■
Habranthus / Rain lily	■			■		■							■
Haemanthus katharinae / Blood lily	■	■										■	■
Hemerocallis / Daylily	■	■	■	■	■			■	■	■	■		■
Hymenocallis / Peruvian daffodil				■		■					■		■
Iris	■	■	■	■	■	■	■	■	■	■	■		■
Lilium / Lily	■	■	■	■	■	■		■	■	■	■		■
Lycoris / Spider lily	■	■		■		■					■		■
Oxalis	■	■		■		■		■					■
Polianthes tuberosa / Tuberose						■					■		■
Sinningia speciosa / Gloxinia	■	■				■	■	■	■	■		■	■

Botanical names / Common names	Pink	Red	Orange	Yellow	Cream	White	Blue	Lavender	Purple	Multicolor	Fragrant	Shade	Container
Sprekelia formosissima / Aztec lily, Jacobean lily		■											■
Tigridia pavonia / Tiger flower, Mexican shell flower	■	■	■	■	■	■				■			■
Tulbaghia								■					■
Vallota speciosa / Scarborough lily	■	■				■						■	■
Watsonia	■	■	■			■			■		■		■
Zantedeschia / Calla, calla lily	■	■	■	■	■	■			■	■		■	■
Zephyranthes / Zephyr flower, fairy lily	■			■		■							■

ASIATIC HYBRID LILIES (Lilium) *rise majestically above border of summer-flowering annuals.*

ELEGANT CALLAS (Zantedeschia elliottiana) *enhance the summer garden with attractive flowers and foliage.*

AUTUMN BLOOM SEASON

Botanical names / Common names	Pink	Red	Orange	Yellow	Cream	White	Blue	Lavender	Purple	Multicolor	Fragrant	Shade	Container
Begonia tuberhybrida / Tuberous begonia	■	■	■	■	■	■				■		■	■
Canna	■	■	■	■	■	■				■			■
Colchicum / Meadow saffron	■					■		■	■				■
Crocus	■					■		■	■	■			■
Cyclamen	■	■				■		■	■			■	■
Dahlia	■	■	■	■	■	■		■	■	■			
Dietes / Fortnight lily, African iris				■		■							■
Gladiolus	■	■	■	■	■	■		■	■	■			
Hemerocallis / Daylily	■	■	■	■	■			■	■	■	■		■
Iris	■	■	■	■	■	■	■	■	■	■	■		
Leucojum / Snowflake	■					■						■	
Lilium / Lily	■	■	■	■	■	■		■	■	■	■		■
Lycoris / Spider lily	■	■		■		■					■		■
Nerine	■	■	■			■							■
Oxalis	■	■		■		■		■					■
Polianthes tuberosa / Tuberose						■					■		■
Schizostylis coccinea / Crimson flag, Kaffir lily	■	■											■
Sternbergia lutea				■									■
Tulbaghia								■					■
Vallota speciosa / Scarborough lily	■	■				■						■	■
Zephyranthes / Zephyr flower, fairy lily	■			■		■							■

LIKE A BREATH OF SPRING in early autumn, Lycoris radiata *displays delicate blossoms above leafless stems.*

WINTER BLOOM SEASON

Botanical names / Common names	Pink	Red	Orange	Yellow	Cream	White	Blue	Lavender	Purple	Multicolor	Fragrant	Shade	Container
Bulbinella floribunda				■	■								
Chionodoxa / Glory-of-the-snow						■	■						
Clivia miniata / Kaffir lily		■	■	■								■	■
Crocus			■	■	■	■	■	■	■	■			■
Cyclamen	■	■				■		■	■			■	■
Dietes / Fortnight lily, African iris				■		■							■
Eranthis hyemalis / Winter aconite				■									
Eucharis grandiflora / Amazon lily						■					■	■	■
Galanthus / Snowdrop						■							
Iris	■	■	■	■		■	■	■	■	■	■		■
Lachenalia / Cape cowslip	■	■	■	■									■
Leucojum / Snowflake	■					■						■	
Narcissus / Daffodil, jonquil				■	■	■				■	■		■
Oxalis	■	■		■		■			■				■
Scilla / Squill	■					■	■		■			■	■
Tulbaghia									■				■
Veltheimia viridifolia	■											■	■

NARCISSUS 'February Gold' sparkles in subdued late winter landscape.

WINTER ACONITE (Eranthis hyemalis) shines brightly through its traditional backdrop: snow.

NATURALIZING BULBS

If you're drawn to the beauty of bulbs but prefer to avoid the rigidity of a formal planting, or if you want to enjoy bulbs in season without obligation to much additional care, then naturalizing should appeal to you. Both in planting and care, nothing could be simpler.

Choose carefully. As a first step in naturalizing, look over the list of suitable bulbs on this page, then read their descriptions (pages 18 to 77). Select those bulbs best suited to your climate and garden conditions. Next, make sure you have an appropriate planting area for your selected bulbs—usually a grassy meadow or lightly shaded woodland, depending on the particular bulb. Pay particular attention to the need for sun or shade, and match the bulb's moisture needs to your climate or your ability to apply water when needed.

Planting guidelines. The traditional naturalizing method is to pick up a handful of bulbs, broadcast them over the desired area, and then plant them where they fall.

To achieve the most realistic effect, you should scatter bulbs so the drift pattern has a greater density at one end or toward the center— as though the bulbs began growing in one location and gradually increased to colonize outlying territory. Be sure to plant the bulbs far enough apart so they can grow well and increase without overcrowding.

Plant at the proper time for your region, setting bulbs at the correct depths (as specified in the individual bulbs' descriptions). Thereafter, you can let nature take over: if you've chosen your bulbs carefully, they'll need little attention from you. You can enhance performance, though, if you apply fertilizer each year just after the blooming period (for more about fertilizers, see pages 86 and 87).

After a number of years, flowers may decrease in size and quantity, signaling overcrowding. When this occurs, it's time to dig, divide, and replant (see directions on pages 88 and 89).

LAVISH SWEEP of daffodils flows through hillside garden in wildflower fashion.

BULBS FOR NATURALIZING

Allium (some species)	Endymion	Leucocoryne
Anemone	Eranthis	Leucojum
Brodiaea	Erythronium	Lilium (some species)
Bulbocodium	Freesia	Muscari
Calochortus	Fritillaria	Narcissus
Camassia	Galanthus	Ornithogalum umbellatum
Chionodoxa	Hyacinthus (some species)	Puschkinia
Colchicum	Ipheion	Scilla
Crocosmia	Ixia	Sparaxis
Crocus	Ixiolirion	Sternbergia
Cyclamen	Lapeirousia	Tulipa (some species)

GROWTH CYCLES

Despite their individual differences, all bulbs follow an annual cycle with periods of growth, bloom, and dormancy. Seasonal timing varies by type of bulb, climate, and time of planting.

Most spring-blooming bulbs are dormant during the coldest months; other varieties are dormant during the dry season. The chart below shows the annual growth cycle of some popular bulbs.

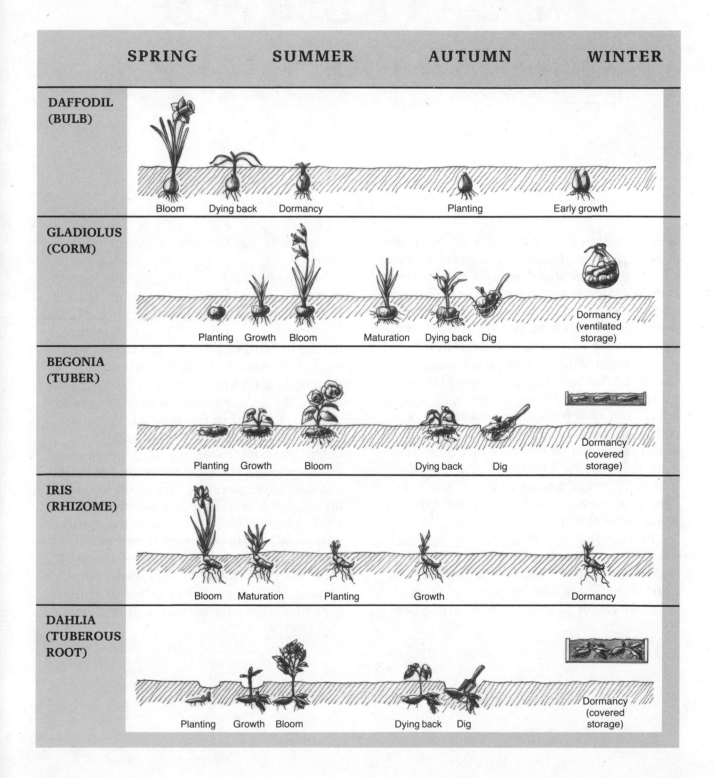

	SPRING	SUMMER	AUTUMN	WINTER

DAFFODIL (BULB): Bloom — Dying back — Dormancy — Planting — Early growth

GLADIOLUS (CORM): Planting — Growth — Bloom — Maturation — Dying back — Dig — Dormancy (ventilated storage)

BEGONIA (TUBER): Planting — Growth — Bloom — Dying back — Dig — Dormancy (covered storage)

IRIS (RHIZOME): Bloom — Maturation — Planting — Growth — Dormancy

DAHLIA (TUBEROUS ROOT): Planting — Growth — Bloom — Dying back — Dig — Dormancy (covered storage)

A CATALOG OF FAVORITE BULBS

In the following 58 pages, you'll find descriptive profiles of well-known, popular bulbs, regional favorites, and lesser known but desirable types that deserve wider recognition. The information given for each bulb will let you evaluate its suitability for your climate and garden conditions.

Each entry opens with a thumbnail sketch of the bulb's appearance and cultural preferences. First, we indicate just what kind of "bulb" it is: true bulb, corm, tuber, rhizome, or tuberous root. Then we note the season or seasons in which the bulb flowers, the blossom color (or colors), and the average height of the tallest species' flowering stems (or the height range from shortest to tallest species).

Planting time is indicated by season; planting location is stated in terms of the necessary type of light—sun, filtered sun, light shade, high shade, part shade, moderate shade, or shade. (For definitions of these terms, see "Where to Plant" on page 83.)

Planting depth is usually given in inches from soil surface to bottom of bulb. But in some cases, bulbs should be planted "even with soil surface"; this means that the tip of bulb or corm or the top of tuber or rhizome should be level with the soil.

The last line gives hardiness (cold tolerance) as an approximate limit to a bulb's outdoor survival in the ground. Because hardiness depends on a number of variables, these temperatures can't be absolutely precise. Planting location, for example, can affect survival: the plant snuggled up against a wall may live through periods when temperatures in exposed areas dip below the hardiness limit. Rapid changes in temperature can also have an effect; if cold comes suddenly after a warm period, a plant may be damaged or killed at temperatures above its usual hardiness limit.

MASSED DAHLIAS put on a striking summertime show in a public garden.

ACHIMENES

Photo on page 22

Type of bulb: Rhizome
Season of bloom: Summer
Colors: Pink, blue, lavender, orchid, purple
Grows to: 1 to 2 feet (some trailing)
When to plant: Late winter or early spring
Where to plant: Light shade
How deep to plant: ½ to 1 inch
Hardiness: Tender; store indoors over winter (see below)

Achimenes puts on a lavish floral display throughout the summer, often blooming so profusely that its slender stems and hairy, pointed oval leaves are almost obscured from view. Each flower is a five-lobed, flat-faced trumpet, 1 to 3 inches across.

Container culture. This plant looks its best when displayed in containers—individual pots, planters, or hanging baskets. Plant the small, irregularly shaped rhizomes in late winter or early spring, maintaining a minimum temperature of 60°F/ 16°C to encourage sprouting. Plant about 1 inch deep in a mixture of half moist peat moss, half sand; when plants are about 3 inches tall, transplant to containers filled with a potting mix of equal parts peat moss, leaf mold, and perlite. Or plant rhizomes directly in their intended containers (using the potting mix just described), setting them ½ to 1 inch deep and 2 to 3 inches apart.

During the growing season, pinch back new growth if you want plump, bushy plants; leave growth unchecked for hanging basket specimens.

Water growing plants regularly. Once a month, apply a liquid fertilizer diluted to half strength. When day length shortens, flowering will lessen, then cease. As blooming ends, gradually cut back on water and let plants die down. Store rhizomes in their containers over winter, keeping soil dry and cool (but not below 40°F/4°C). In late winter or early spring, knock rhizomes out of containers and replant.

AGAPANTHUS

LILY-OF-THE-NILE

Photo on page 22

Type of bulb: Rhizome with fleshy roots
Season of bloom: Summer
Colors: White, blue
Grows to: 1 to 5 feet
When to plant: Spring or summer (from containers); early spring or autumn (from divisions)
Where to plant: Sun; part or light shade where summers are hot
How deep to plant: Juncture of leaf bases and rhizomes ½ inch beneath soil surface
Hardiness: Evergreen types to about 20°F/ − 7°C; deciduous types to about 10°F/ − 12°C; in colder regions, grow as a container plant

The blue or white blossoms of *Agapanthus* bring a welcome touch of coolness to the summer garden. Depending on the species and variety, height of flowering stems ranges from 1 to 5 feet, but all plants are built along the same lines: thick stems, each topped by a rounded cluster of tubular to bell-shaped blooms, rise from fountainlike clumps of strap-shaped leaves (evergreen, with two exceptions).

The two most commonly sold species are *A. orientalis* and *A. africanus*, both also offered under the name *A. umbellatus*. To confuse matters further, *A. orientalis* is often sold as *A. africanus*. If you're intent on purchasing a particular species, buy blooming plants and check the appearance of the flower clusters carefully (see descriptions below).

A. orientalis is the tallest *Agapanthus*, with the broadest leaves and the greatest number of flowers (up to 100) per cluster. Some nurseries sell named selections in white and various shades of light to fairly dark blue; 'Flore Pleno' has double blue blossoms. More often, however, you'll find plants labeled only as "white" or "blue." If you're after a particular shade of blue, choose plants while they're in bloom.

Narrower leaves, shorter stems (to about 1½ feet) and fewer flowers per cluster (up to 30) characterize *A. africanus*. Flower color is deep blue.

The deciduous species, *A. inapertus,* is as tall and as many-flowered as *A. orientalis,* but the deep blue, tubular blossoms are pendant from atop the stems.

For foreground plantings, choose from several shorter named varieties. Deciduous 'Queen Anne' has narrow leaves in clumps to 15 inches high; stems grow to about 2 feet. Flowers are medium blue. White-blossomed 'Rancho White' is in the same size range, but its leaves are broader. You may find it sold simply as 'Rancho' or 'Dwarf White'. 'Peter Pan' is generally the shortest of the dwarf types, with foliage under a foot high and blue flowers carried on 1 to 1½-foot stems. However, there's some variation in height and in the size of foliage and flowers, since some 'Peter Pan' plants are raised from seed rather than division.

Uses. Both evergreen and deciduous kinds of *Agapanthus* are attractive foliage plants when not in bloom; when they're in flower, their cool blue and white blossoms provide refreshing contrast to yellow and orange summer-flowering plants. Use the larger kinds as accent clumps or in mass or border plantings. Smaller varieties are fine for foreground accents and pathway plants.

Garden culture. Where summers are cool or mild, choose a planting area in full sun; in hot regions, plants need light shade all day (or at least some shade during the heat of the afternoon). *Agapanthus* tolerates heavy soils and will put up with infrequent watering once it's established, but for best performance, give these plants good, well-drained soil and regular watering throughout the growth and flowering season. Set out nursery plants about 1½ feet apart, with the juncture of leaf bases and rhizomes ½ inch beneath the soil surface. (*Agapanthus* is sold only in containers.)

Divide infrequently, only when clumps show a decline in vigor and flower quality—perhaps every 6 years. Early spring is the best time to divide all types, though evergreen *Agapanthus* can also be divided in autumn.

Container culture. All types of *Agapanthus* perform best when crowding the container to capacity. Follow directions "C" on page 91. Where winters are too cold for outdoor survival, move containers to a sheltered location where plants will receive some light and temperatures will remain above freezing.

ALLIUM

DRUMSTICKS
GOLDEN GARLIC
STAR OF PERSIA

Photos on pages 2 and 22

Type of bulb: True bulb

Season of bloom: Spring, summer

Colors: Pink, red, violet, lavender, blue, yellow, white

Grows to: 6 inches to over 5 feet

When to plant: Autumn or spring

Where to plant: Sun

How deep to plant: 2 to 4 inches, depending on size of bulb

Hardiness: To about −30°F/−35°C; to about −10°F/−23°C for *A. neapolitanum*

Though they often don't realize it, most people are acquainted with certain alliums—the culinary staples onions and garlic, as well as shallots, chives, and leeks. All species bear compact or loose rounded clusters of small flowers at the tops of leafless stems. The tallest types reach 5 feet or more, while the shortest top out under 1 foot; between these extremes are many of intermediate height.

Summer-blooming giant allium, *A. giganteum,* is the skyscraper of the group. Its softball-size clusters of lavender blossoms are borne on 5 to 6-foot stalks; leaves are a modest 1½ feet long. Nearly as tall are *A. elatum* and *A. rosenbachianum,* both violet-flowered species that bloom in late spring. Spring-flowering *A. aflatunense* also resembles *A. giganteum,* but its stems are shorter (3 to 5 feet) and its heads of lilac blossoms are smaller.

Among the alliums of middling size are three strikingly colored species, all blooming in summer. *A. atropurpureum* and *A. sphaerocephalum* (commonly called "drumsticks") both grow 2 to 2½ feet tall and bear 2-inch flower clusters; the former produces blossoms of dark purple to nearly black, while the latter has very tight clusters of red purple blossoms. *A. pulchellum* also has red purple flowers, but its stems reach only 2 feet at the tallest.

The under-2-foot category offers the greatest variety of colors and floral forms. *A. christophii* (star of Persia) blooms in late spring, bearing the largest flower clusters of all *Alliums*—6 to 12 inches across. The star-shaped blooms vary from lilac to amethyst purple. Stems are 1 to 1½ feet tall; the 1½-foot-long leaves have silvery white undersides.

Four other worthwhile small species also flower in late spring. *A. caeruleum,* the blue allium, has cornflower blue blossoms in 2-inch rounded clusters on 1 to 1½-foot-tall stems. Rose pink *A. roseum* bears its 4-inch flower clusters on 12 to 14-inch stems. The shortest of these late spring bloomers is *A. ostrowskianum;* its stems are just 8 to 12 inches tall, topped with 2-inch clusters of rose colored flowers. Its carmine red variety 'Zwanenburg' is only about 6 inches tall. For color contrast in the late spring group, choose *A. moly,* the golden garlic. Loose 2 to 3-inch clusters of bright yellow blossoms appear atop 9 to 18-inch stems; the gray green leaves are nearly as long as the stems.

Midspring flowers are provided by *A. karataviense,* the Turkestan allium. Its 5-inch clusters of pinkish beige to reddish lilac blossoms are carried on 8 to 12-inch stems. Each plant usually produces two purple-tinted leaves, each up to 4 inches wide and nearly prostrate.

Pure white *A. neapolitanum,* another midspring bloomer, has loose 3-inch flower clusters; stems are about 1 foot tall, rising above 1-inch-wide leaves. *A. n.* 'Grandiflorum' (and its form 'Cowanii') have larger individual flowers and begin blooming a bit earlier. *A. neapolitanum* and its varieties are hardy only to about −10°F/−23°C, but will survive from year to year in colder regions if grown in containers (see directions "C" on page 91).

Uses. The tall and middle-size species provide attractive accents in mixed groupings of annuals and perennials. Shorter species are useful in foreground drifts or clumps and as pathway edgings. *A. caeruleum, A. moly,* and *A. neapolitanum* are the best choices for naturalizing.

Garden culture. All ornamental alliums prefer well-drained soil (preferably on the sandy side), enriched before planting with organic matter. Plant bulbs as deep as their height or width, whichever is greater. Space smaller species 4 to 6 inches apart, larger ones 8 to 12 inches apart. Water regularly during the growth and bloom period, but when foliage begins to yellow after flowering, water less often or even let soil go dry. Leave plantings undisturbed until vigor and flower quality decline due to overcrowding. At that time, dig clumps after foliage has died down, divide bulbs, and replant in late summer or early autumn. If replanting in the same plot, dig plenty of organic matter into the soil.

ALSTROEMERIA

PERUVIAN LILY

Photo on page 9

Type of bulb: Tuberous root

Season of bloom: Spring, summer

Colors: Red, orange, yellow, cream, white, pink, lavender

Grows to: 2 to 4 feet

When to plant: Winter (bare root), spring (from containers)

Where to plant: Sun; filtered sun or part shade where summers are hot

How deep to plant: 4 inches

Hardiness: To about 20°F/−7°C; to about 0°F/−18°C with winter protection (see page 89)

Alstroemeria's airy sprays of azalea-like flowers enliven the garden as spring slips into summer. Viewed individually, young plants look rather wispy, so it's best to set them out in groups. As clumps become established, the leafy upright stems multiply, giving the planting a bulkier look.

(Continued on page 23)

Amaryllis belladonna

Anemone coronaria

Agapanthus orientalis

Achimenes *'Minette'*

Allium moly

The Peruvian lilies sold in nurseries are usually hybrid strains (primarily Ligtu Hybrids and Chilean Hybrids); these come in the range of colors listed on page 21. For guaranteed orange or yellow, look for *A. aurantiaca* and its variety 'Lutea'. All types of *Alstroemeria* go dormant in summer or autumn; the Ligtu Hybrids die back to the ground in summer, but *A. aurantiaca* may remain green until the first hard frost.

Uses. *Alstroemeria* provides a showy display for weeks during late spring and summer. It's best used in a mixed planting, though—the plants die back to the ground after the bloom period, leaving bare patches that must be concealed by the foliage of other plants.

Garden culture. Peruvian lilies appreciate well-drained soil enriched with organic matter before planting. The ideal location is a spot where roots will be in cool, moist soil during the growing season, while flowering stems receive sun (in cool to moderate climates) or filtered sunlight or part shade (where summers are hot). Mulch the planting area to keep soil cool and moist, or overplant it with nonaggressive ground cover annuals or perennials such as verbena or sweet alyssum.

Choose a site where plants can remain undisturbed for years. Plantings spread in time but usually don't need dividing, and plants re-establish slowly after replanting.

Tuberous roots may be sold bare root from late autumn through winter; they're brittle, so handle with extreme care. Space roots about a foot apart, planting so the growth node is about 4 inches beneath the soil surface. Carefully spread out roots as you plant; in time, they'll grow to a considerable depth.

During the growing season, some nurseries also sell young plants in 1 or 2-gallon containers, ready for planting.

Water *Alstroemeria* regularly during the growing and blooming season, keeping water off flower heads to prevent stems from toppling. As flowers fade and plants enter their dormant period, water less often. Be sure to protect growing plants from slugs and snails.

Container culture. Follow directions "B" on page 91, using large, deep wooden boxes or tubs.

AMARYLLIS belladonna

*BELLADONNA LILY
NAKED LADY*

Photo on page 22

Type of bulb: True bulb
Season of bloom: Late summer
Color: Pink
Grows to: 2 to 3 feet
When to plant: Late summer, immediately after bloom
Where to plant: Sun
How deep to plant: Top of bulb neck even with or just above soil surface (where temperatures remain above 15°F/−9°C); 6 inches deep (in colder regions)
Hardiness: To about 15°F/−9°C; to about −20°F/−29°C with winter protection (see page 89)
NOTE: *Hippeastrum* is also called "amaryllis."

This sturdy plant's dark green, strap-shaped leaves form good-looking, fountainlike clumps about 1 foot high and 2 feet wide. Foliage dies down in late spring or early summer; wine red 2 to 3-foot flower stalks rise from bare earth about 6 weeks later. Each stalk bears a cluster of four to twelve blossoms, trumpet-shaped and highly fragrant. Medium rose pink is the most common color, but paler and deeper variations exist.

Uses. Because of its tall, bare flower stems, amaryllis is best planted among lower growing perennials that will mask its leaflessness.

Garden culture. Amaryllis isn't particular about soil type, but it does require fairly good drainage. Plant bulbs immediately after the blooming season ends. Where winter temperatures remain above 15°F/−9°C, set bulbs about 1 foot apart, keeping tops of bulb necks at or slightly above the soil line. In colder areas, plant about 6 inches deep and in a southern exposure, even against a south-facing wall. Established

plants are quite tolerant of drought, though performance is better if they receive regular watering while in leaf.

Divide and replant amaryllis infrequently. Crowded conditions don't hamper bloom, and reset plants may not bloom for a year or two while they re-establish.

ANEMONE

WINDFLOWER

Photo on page 22

Type of bulb: Tuber; rhizome (*A. apennina*)
Season of bloom: Spring
Colors: Purple, blue, red, pink, white
Grows to: 3 to 18 inches
When to plant: Autumn; early spring for *A. coronaria* and *A. fulgens* where winter temperatures fall below 0°F/−18°C
Where to plant: Sun, part shade, or light shade
How deep to plant: 1 to 2 inches
Hardiness: Varies (see below)

"Bright" and "cheerful" are two adjectives often applied to anemones. And with good reason: their clear, vivid colors seem to capture the essence of springtime. The most widely available types can be separated into two groups, based on size, hardiness, and uses.

Daisylike flowers and stems no taller than 8 inches characterize rhizomatous *A. apennina* and tuberous *A. blanda*. These are the hardy anemones, able to withstand temperatures of −10°F/−23°C (or lower, if protected with a winter mulch)—and in fact, both need winter chill for good performance. Bloom begins in early spring; *A. blanda* flowers several weeks before *A. apennina*. Both species have clumps of fernlike or parsleylike foliage and blue flowers—sky blue and upward facing in *A. apennina*, darker blue and nodding in *A. blanda*. Each also has varieties with white and pink blossoms.

The second group of anemones includes the taller, more frequently planted tuberous types with poppylike and double flowers. These are less hardy, able to remain in the ground only where temperatures remain above 0°F/−18°C. The poppy-flowered anemone, *A. coronaria*, has finely divided foliage and leafy stems to 1½ feet tall. Each stem bears one 1½ to 2½-inch-wide blossom—red, pink, white, or blue, usually with blue stamens. The DeCaen strain of *A. coronaria* produces single flowers; the St. Brigid strain has semidouble and double flowers.

A. fulgens, the scarlet wind-flower, grows to 1 foot tall; it bears brilliant red, black-centered blossoms up to 2½ inches across. The St. Bavo strain includes pink, rusty coral, and terra cotta in addition to red.

Uses. The smaller anemones, *A. apennina* and *A. blanda,* work well as ground cover drifts beneath deciduous shrubs and trees, as underplanting for tulips, or naturalized in short grass.

A. coronaria and *A. fulgens* are good for colorful mass plantings, as accent clumps in borders of spring flowers, and as container plants.

Garden culture. All anemones need well-drained soil liberally amended with organic matter before planting. Plant tubers (or rhizomes) top side up, 1 to 2 inches deep and 4 inches apart. (Identifying the top side of tubers and rhizomes is often difficult, due to their irregular shapes. Look for the depressed scar left by the base of the last year's stem; the scarred side of the tuber is the top.)

Plant *A. apennina* and *A. blanda* in autumn; where winter temperatures drop below −10°F/−23°C, apply winter protection annually after the first hard frost. These two can be left undisturbed for many years to form large colonies; dig and divide only when vigor and bloom quality decline.

Plant *A. coronaria* and *A. fulgens* in autumn where they're hardy in the ground; in colder regions, plant in early spring. Water plants regularly throughout the growth and blooming season, then withhold all water when foliage yellows.

In dry-summer regions where tubers are hardy in the ground, you can leave them in place from one year to the next. But where there's summer watering or summer rainfall, and in areas where winter lows dip below 0°F/−18°C, dig tubers when foliage yellows and store as for *Begonia.*

Container culture. For *A. coronaria, A. blanda,* and *A. fulgens,* follow directions "B" on page 91.

BABIANA

BABOON FLOWER

Photo on page 27

Type of bulb: Corm
Season of bloom: Mid to late spring
Colors: Blue, lavender, purple, red, cream, white
Grows to: 6 to 12 inches
When to plant: Autumn; early spring where winter temperatures fall below 20°F/−7°C
Where to plant: Sun or part shade
How deep to plant: 4 inches
Hardiness: To 20°F/−7°C; in colder regions, dig and store over winter as for *Gladiolus*

Clear, rich colors—sometimes almost fluorescent—are a babiana trademark. Six or more blossoms appear on each flowering stem; each bloom is up to 2 inches across, shaped like a shallow cup with six equal segments. Leaves are borne in fans, like those of gladiolus. They're hairy and sword shaped, with lengthwise ribbing.

B. stricta (and its varieties) and the striking *B. rubrocyanea* are the most widely sold forms. *B. stricta* has 1-foot-tall stems; *B. rubrocyanea* grows just half that size and bears red-throated royal blue blossoms.

Uses. Plant babiana to be viewed at close range—in rock gardens, along pathways, in foreground drifts.

Garden culture. Choose well-drained soil, in a location that receives sun for at least half the day. For a massed effect, set corms 4 inches deep and 4 to 6 inches apart.

Water regularly throughout the growing and flowering period; taper off as foliage yellows after bloom. Trim foliage off after it dies back.

Where corms can winter in the ground, leave them in place for several years—they'll increase and bloom more profusely each year. In colder climates, dig and store as for *Gladiolus.*

Container culture. Plant corms in a deep pot, about 1 inch deep and 1 inch apart. Follow directions "B" on page 91.

BEGONIA tuberhybrida

TUBEROUS BEGONIA

Photo on page 7

Type of bulb: Tuber
Season of bloom: Summer, autumn
Colors: Red, orange, yellow, pink, cream, white, multicolor
Grows to: 1 to 1½ feet
When to plant: Late winter to late spring, depending on climate
Where to plant: Filtered sun or light shade
How deep to plant: Just beneath soil surface
Hardiness: Tender; store indoors over winter (see below)

For general magnificence and great range of color and pattern, tuberous begonias are second to no other summer-flowering bulb. And for number of blossoms to size of plant, they clearly lead the pack. In addition to refining colors and patterns, hybridizers have tailored flower form. A number of modern varieties have blossoms that mimic those of other plants: you'll find blooms resembling roses, camellias, and carnations.

Well-grown plants may reach a height of 1 to 1½ feet and produce flowers the size of saucers. The irregularly shaped, pointed leaves grow to about 8 inches long. A special group of hybrids, sometimes sold as *B. t.* 'Pendula', have drooping stems and downward-facing flowers. These are plants for hanging baskets, best displayed at eye level.

Uses. Tuberous begonias accent shady summer gardens; they're effective in mass plantings or mixed groupings.

Culture. Despite the claims of some frustrated gardeners, tuberous begonias are not inherently difficult to grow. But neither will they tolerate neglect: to achieve a spectacular display, you'll need to satisfy all their cultural needs. The one variable beyond the gardener's control—and one that can strongly influence success or failure—is climate. Tuberous begonias revel in moist air and "tepid" temperatures: not too hot, but not too cool. In the United States, the best regions are those where night temperatures remain above 60°F/16°C—along the Pacific and North Atlantic coasts, in Great Lakes coastal areas, and in northern Minnesota and Michigan. The most trying conditions are heat plus high humidity, typical of Southeast and Gulf Coast summers.

Though tubers may be available as early as midwinter, the right time to plant depends on your climate: plants can go outdoors as soon as night temperatures are sure to remain at or above 50°F/10°C.

For the longest possible bloom season, start tubers indoors 6 to 8 weeks before the outdoor planting time. If you're planting a number of tubers, it's easiest to start them in a flat or shallow box, spacing them about 4 inches apart. Use a porous, moisture-retentive rooting medium: three parts leaf mold, compost, or peat moss mixed with one part builder's sand. Set in tubers indented side up, covering them with no more than ¼ inch of rooting medium. Then place the flat in a well-lit spot (but not in direct sun) where temperatures will remain above 65°F/18°C. Keep the rooting medium moist but not saturated during the rooting period.

When the tubers have produced two leaves, you can pot them up and, if outdoor temperatures are warm enough, take them outside. The potting mixture should be moisture retentive but fast draining; a typical mix contains equal parts peat moss or ground bark, leaf mold, and builder's sand. Choose containers large enough to leave 2 inches between all sides of the tubers and the container edges.

Some gardeners prefer to mass tuberous begonias in planters rather than potting them individually, or even to set them directly in the ground under high-branching trees. For in-ground planting, mix the existing soil with potting mix in a 1:2 ratio. Leaves on sprouted tubers all point in one direction, and when flowers come, they'll also face that way. When planting, remember to "face" plants so you'll see the fronts of the flowers.

Tuberous begonias need protection from wind but freely circulating air: still, moist air will lead to mildewed foliage. Plenty of light (but no direct sun) is another requirement. Choose a spot in filtered sun or light shade—under high-branching trees, on the east or north side of house, wall, or fence, or under light-modifying overhead structures of lath, shade cloth, or fiberglass.

As plants grow, keep soil moist but not soggy. Too much water will cause tubers to rot; too little will check growth. In dry climates, you'll also need to raise humidity around plants—set up a permanent mist or fog system, or use such attachments on your hose. Except for misting, however, keep water off leaves and flowers: the weight of the water droplets can topple blooming plants or break their stems.

Begin applications of liquid fertilizer a week or two after young plants have been transplanted from the starting flat. Gardeners who are going for the largest possible blossoms use a half-strength solution every other week, but you can easily grow fine plants with monthly regular-strength applications.

In late summer to mid-autumn, flower production will slow and then cease. When you notice this slowdown, stop fertilizing and cut back on water, keeping soil just moist enough to prevent foliage from wilting (you want tubers to store as much food as possible before they enter dormancy). When leaves begin to turn yellow, withhold water. If frosts are likely to occur before plants die down completely, move containers into a well-lit, frost-free location.

When leaves fall off and stems separate easily from tubers, the tubers are ready for storage. Place containers in a cool, dark spot where temperatures will remain above freezing (preferably between 40°F/4°C and 50°F/10°C). You can also store tubers out of their containers. Knock them from their pots, remove stems and all soil, and let them dry for 3 days in the sun. Then store as directed under "covered storage" on page 89.

For begonias planted in the ground, withhold water and fertilizer as directed above; dig tubers before the first frost, then dry and store as for container-grown plants.

BELAMCANDA chinensis

BLACKBERRY LILY

Photo on page 27

Type of bulb: Rhizome
Season of bloom: Summer
Color: Orange
Grows to: 2 to 3 feet
When to plant: Autumn; early spring where winter temperatures fall below 10°F/−12°C
Where to plant: Sun or light shade
How deep to plant: Just beneath soil surface
Hardiness: To about 10°F/−12°C; to about −10°F/−23°C with winter protection (see page 89)

Blackberry lily bears 2-inch, red-spotted orange blossoms, carried on 2 to 3-foot branching stems that rise from irislike fans of foliage. Though each bloom lasts just one day, each slender stem produces numerous flowers over a period of several weeks. When seed capsules mature in autumn, they split open to reveal clusters of shining black seeds resembling blackberries.

Hybrids between *Belamcanda* and *Pardanthopsis*—called *Pardancanda*—resemble blackberry lily in appearance and cultural requirements. Their flowers come in a greater range of colors, though: you'll find blooms in blue and purple, yellow, and pink as well as in orange.

(Continued on next page)

Uses. Blackberry lily is a good accent plant; its vertical foliage and bright blooms add interest to plantings of annuals or perennials.

Garden culture. Plant rhizomes in well-drained soil; space them 1 foot apart, with their tops just beneath the soil surface. Water plants regularly during the growing and blooming season; after flowering, they'll get by with less frequent watering.

Established clumps give the best display, so divide and reset infrequently.

BLETILLA striata

CHINESE GROUND ORCHID

Photo on page 27

Type of bulb: Rhizome
Season of bloom: Late spring
Colors: Lavender, white
Grows to: 1½ to 2 feet
When to plant: Autumn to early spring; winter (from divisions)
Where to plant: Part shade or filtered sun
How deep to plant: 1 inch
Hardiness: To about 20°F/−7°C; to about 10°F/−12°C with winter protection (see page 89)

Easy-to-grow *Bletilla* is unmistakably an orchid—its 2-inch flowers look much like the cattleya orchids of corsage fame. The typical color is lavender, but a white-flowered variety 'Alba' is sometimes available.

Plants break dormancy in early spring, sending up lance-shaped, plaited-looking light green leaves—three to six per plant. Bare flower stems to about 2 feet tall follow in late spring; each produces three to seven blossoms, spaced apart from each other toward the stem end.

Uses. Plant *Bletilla* in a lightly shaded spot, setting out bulbs in clumps, patches, or drifts. The delicate blooms look especially attractive in combination with rhododendrons or azaleas.

Garden culture. Set out rhizomes about 1 inch deep and 1 foot apart in good, well-drained soil enriched with organic matter before planting. When leaves emerge, put out bait for slugs and snails. Water regularly throughout the growing and blooming season, but taper off watering when leaves begin to yellow in autumn. After foliage has died back completely, rhizomes enter a dormant period; during this time, they don't need much water.

Large, crowded clumps give the best display of blooms, but you may dig and divide as needed during winter dormancy.

BRODIAEA

ITHURIEL'S SPEAR

Photo on page 27

Type of bulb: Corm
Season of bloom: Spring, summer
Colors: Blue, purple, lavender, yellow, white
Grows to: 10 to 30 inches
When to plant: Autumn
Where to plant: Sun
How deep to plant: 2 to 3 inches
Hardiness: To about −10°F/−23°C

In recent years, botanists have transferred a number of species from *Brodiaea* to *Dichelostemma* and *Triteleia*. But since nurseries often still offer these species as *Brodiaea*, they are listed as such here. Alternative new names are given in parentheses. For the plant once called *Brodiaea uniflora* (spring star flower), see *Ipheion uniflorum* on page 50.

The brodiaeas (and former brodiaeas) are native to the western United States, where they experience a hot, dry, and usually long summer dormant period. In the wild, these are field and meadow plants, often waving their heads of blue, white, or yellow flowers above or among the dry grasses of fields and hillsides. Each plant produces a few grasslike leaves and a single slender stem topped by a loose cluster of bell-shaped or funnel-shaped blossoms.

B. capitata (*Dichelostemma pulchellum*) blooms in early to midspring, producing tight clusters of deep blue to violet flowers on 2-foot stems. Harvest brodiaea, *B. coronaria*, bears 1-inch-long dark blue blossoms on 10-inch stems in late spring and early summer. Very similar, but a bit taller and larger flowered, is *B. elegans*—which may be sold as *B. grandiflora* or even as *B. coronaria*.

B. hyacinthina, *B. lactea*, and *B. lilacina* have all been regrouped under *Triteleia hyacinthina*. These forms have stems up to 2½ feet tall; the open clusters of bell-shaped white flowers (or lavender, in the case of *B. lilacina*) bloom in early to midsummer.

B. ixioides (*Triteleia ixioides*), commonly called golden brodiaea, is a late spring bloomer with inch-long yellow flowers on 1-foot stems. Ithuriel's spear, *B. laxa* (*Triteleia laxa*), blooms in mid to late spring; its many-flowered clusters of bluish purple blossoms are carried on stems up to 2½ feet tall. Individual flowers reach nearly 2 inches long. *Brodiaea* 'Queen Fabiola' (*Triteleia* 'Queen Fabiola') is frequently sold as a selected form of this species.

Uses. *Brodiaea* is a good choice for naturalizing at garden fringes and at the edges of uncultivated property. It can also be used to lend a wild-flower-type accent to groupings of other drought-tolerant plants.

Garden culture. Under "native" conditions—hot, absolutely dry summer weather—*Brodiaea* will accept heavy as well as light and well-drained soil. But if summer moisture is inevitable, well-drained soil is a necessity—and even then, there's no guarantee of success. If you live in a moist-summer region and want to try growing *Brodiaea* in the garden, *B. hyacinthina* (*Triteleia hyacinthina*) is probably your best bet. Container culture (see below) is another option. All species need regular watering during their winter and spring growing period. Digging and dividing are necessary only infrequently, when clumps show a decline in vigor and bloom quality.

Container culture. The various species of *Brodiaea* aren't difficult to grow in containers, though they have a rather wispy appearance. Follow directions "B" on page 91.

Babiana stricta

Bulbinella floribunda

Brodiaea elegans

Bletilla striata

Belamcanda chinensis

BULBINELLA floribunda

Photo on page 27

Type of bulb: Rhizome with tuberous roots
Season of bloom: Winter
Colors: Yellow, cream
Grows to: 2 to 3 feet
When to plant: Autumn
Where to plant: Sun; part shade where summers are hot
How deep to plant: Just beneath soil surface
Hardiness: To about 20°F/−7°C

Flowering stems rise from 2-foot fountains of coarse, grasslike leaves; each stem is topped with a 4-inch spike crowded with small, bell-shaped blossoms.

Uses. Plant *Bulbinella* where you need a foliage accent, or use it to provide winter flower color in a location that doesn't receive regular watering in summer.

Garden culture. Set rhizomes just beneath the surface of well-drained soil, spacing them 1 to 1½ feet apart. Water regularly during the growth and flowering period, then taper off watering as foliage dies back in summer. Divide clumps only when overcrowded; resetting causes a decline in vigor and bloom quality.

CALADIUM hortulanum

FANCY-LEAFED CALADIUM
Photo on page 30

Type of bulb: Tuber
Season of bloom: Summer foliage; blooms unimportant
Colors: Patterned foliage in combinations of red, pink, white, green, silver, bronze
Grows to: 2 to 3 feet
When to plant: Early spring
Where to plant: Light shade or filtered sun
How deep to plant: Top of tuber even with soil surface
Hardiness: Tender; dig and store indoors over winter as for *Begonia*

No one would look twice at a caladium flower, which resembles a small calla (*Zantedeschia*). What these plants provide is crowd-stopping foliage. Numerous slim leaf stalks sprout from each tuber; each stalk supports a thin-textured leaf shaped like an elongated heart, up to 1 foot wide and 1½ feet long when well grown. Patterns and color arrangements are almost too varied to describe: veining, dotting, splashing, washing, and edging are some of the ways in which one color may be contrasted against another.

For best performance, caladiums need rich soil, high humidity, heat, plenty of water, and bright light (but not direct sun). In all parts of the country but Florida and some areas of the Gulf Coast, these conditions are easiest to provide if you grow plants in containers.

Uses. Pots of these bright-leafed plants often decorate terraces and patios; they're greenhouse favorites, too. To simulate garden planting, you can sink potted caladiums into the ground.

Garden culture. Choose a spot in light shade or filtered sun; then replace the top 6 inches of soil with the mix recommended for container-grown *Begonia*. Set out plants already started, spacing them 8 to 12 inches apart and keeping tops of tubers even with the soil surface.

Keep soil moist, but not soggy, watering more generously as more leaves develop. Mist foliage daily, using a fine spray of water. Every other week, apply a liquid fertilizer diluted to half strength. Put out bait for slugs and snails. Remove any blossoms that appear; they'll divert energies from leaf production.

When leaves begin to die down in late summer or early autumn, cut back on watering. After foliage has yellowed, dig tubers and store as for *Begonia*.

Container culture. Caladiums need a growing season at least 4 months long, with daytime temperatures above 70°F/21°C. Start tubers indoors a month before outside temperatures normally reach 70°F/21°C. For procedures and soil mixture, see *Begonia*.

CALOCHORTUS

FAIRY LANTERN
GLOBE TULIP
MARIPOSA LILY
STAR TULIP

Type of bulb: True bulb
Season of bloom: Spring, early summer
Colors: White, cream, yellow, lilac, purple, pink, red, multicolors
Grows to: 4 inches to 3 feet
When to plant: Autumn
Where to plant: Sun or light shade
How deep to plant: 3 to 4 inches
Hardiness: To about 10°F/−12°C

Among bulbous plants, *Calochortus* ranks near the top for delicacy and floral beauty. However, the various *Calochortus* species are also among the more challenging to accommodate in the garden, since they demand the long, warm, dry summer that they have in their native habitats in western North America.

Sparse, grasslike foliage is common to all members of this genus, but flower forms can be divided into three distinct groups. Globe tulips or fairy lanterns have three to twenty nodding flowers to each stalk; petals turn inward to form a globe. Star tulips have upward-facing, cup-shaped flowers, with petal tips often rolled outward; those with long, straight hairs on the inner flower parts are called cat's ears or pussy ears. Mariposa lilies are in general the tallest types, with striking cup or bowl-shaped flowers.

Bulb specialists may offer various species, representing some or all of the three basic flower types. Among the globe tulips are *C. albus* (white), *C. amabilis* (yellow), and *C. amoenus* (rosy purple). Star tulips and cat's ears include *C. nudus* (white or lavender), *C. tolmiei* (white or cream, tinged with purple), and *C. uniflorus* (lilac). Most variable of the mariposa lilies is *C. venustus*; its blossoms may be white, pink, light to dark red, purple, or yellow, usually with contrasting markings in the flower center and sometimes extending out onto the petals. Other mariposa lilies are *C. clavatus* and

C. luteus (yellow), *C. splendens* (lilac with purple), *C. nuttallii* (white with purple), and *C. vestae* (white, lilac, or pink, with a contrasting color in the flower center).

Uses. Where conditions favor success in the ground, all *Calochortus* species can be conversation piece ornaments in rock garden plantings or naturalized on sunny, grassy hillsides. As container plants, they're striking in bloom, but foliage is rather wispy.

Garden culture. To grow *Calochortus* successfully, provide well-drained soil, and don't water at all from the time leaves start to yellow after flowering until midautumn (when rainfall begins in native habitats). Set bulbs 3 to 4 inches deep, about 6 inches apart. In the right climates, plantings may remain undisturbed for years.

If you'd like to grow *Calochortus* but don't live in a dry-summer region, try digging bulbs as soon as leaves turn yellow, then holding them in dry sand until autumn. Some gardeners have successfully used this method to grow these plants year after year. An alternative is container culture; be sure to keep soil completely dry during the long summer dormant period.

Container culture. Follow directions "B" on page 91.

CAMASSIA

CAMASS

Photo on page 30

Type of bulb: True bulb
Season of bloom: Spring
Colors: Blue, cream, white
Grows to: 1 to 4 feet
When to plant: Autumn
Where to plant: Sun or light shade
How deep to plant: 3 to 4 inches
Hardiness: To about −35°F/−38°C

You don't grow camass for flamboyant, show-stopping floral displays. Instead, it offers the charm of a meadow wildflower—which is just what it is. Rosettes of grasslike to strap-shaped leaves send up slender spikes of loosely spaced, starlike blossoms; after flowering, foliage dies down completely for the summer dormant period.

Bulb specialists offer several species and varieties of camass. *C. cusickii* bears blue flowers on stems up to 3 feet tall. *C. leichtlinii*, the tallest camass, reaches a height of 4 feet; its blossoms are creamy white. *C. l. suksdorfii* is blue-flowered, while 'Alba' is nearer to white than the species. *C. l.* 'Plena' has double greenish white blossoms. For deep blue blooms, choose *C. quamash* or its varieties 'Orion' and 'San Juan Form'; stems reach about 2½ feet.

Uses. Though camass is at home in meadowlike situations, the tall flower spikes also look attractive in mixed plantings of spring flowers. Since plants die down after bloom, set camass where other plants' foliage will hide its yellowing leaves (and fill in the bare spots left after leaves are entirely gone).

Garden culture. Camass never requires digging and dividing, so choose a planting area where bulbs can remain undisturbed for years.

In autumn, plant the large bulbs 6 inches apart and 3 to 4 inches deep in good, moisture-retentive soil. Plants like ample water during the growing and blooming season, but can get by with less during the summer dormant period.

CANNA

CANNA

Photo on page 30

Type of bulb: Rhizome
Season of bloom: Summer, autumn
Colors: Red, orange, yellow, pink, cream, white, bicolors
Grows to: 1½ to 6 feet
When to plant: Early spring
Where to plant: Sun
How deep to plant: 2 to 4 inches
Hardiness: To about 0°F/−18°C; in colder regions, dig and store over winter as for *Begonia*

For showiness and productivity, you can't go wrong with cannas. You can choose from several heights and a wide range of flower colors, and there's even some variation in foliage—leaves may be green, bronze, or variegated. Rhizomes grow into clumps that produce upright stems sheathed in broad, lance-shaped leaves of decidedly tropical appearance. Each stem bears a spike of large, bright flowers that resemble irregularly shaped gladiolus.

Virtually all cannas in the nursery trade are hybrids of mixed ancestry. The old-fashioned garden favorites grow 4 to 6 feet tall, but lower growing, more compact strains are also available today. The Grand Opera strain, for example, grows a bit over 2 feet tall, while the Pfitzer Dwarf strain reaches a height of 2½ to 3 feet. Shortest of all is the 1½-foot-tall Seven Dwarfs strain; it's usually sold as seeds (follow package directions for planting).

Uses. Cannas are particularly dramatic as color accents, but their bright blossoms and bold leaves also add a striking tropical touch to the garden. They make stunning container plants, too.

Garden culture. Cannas thrive in good, moist soil and a hot, bright location. Choose a sunny area where plants can receive regular watering; incorporate a generous amount of organic matter into the soil before setting out rhizomes.

Where rhizomes are hardy in the ground, plant after the normal last-frost date in spring. Space rhizomes 1½ to 2 feet apart; cover with 2 to 4 inches of soil. In colder regions, start rhizomes indoors (see *Begonia*) a month to 6 weeks before the usual last-frost date so plants will bloom sooner after being planted outdoors.

During the growing and blooming season, give plants plenty of water. As each stem finishes flowering, cut it to the ground; new stems will continue to grow throughout summer and early autumn.

Where the climate is mild enough for cannas to remain planted from year to year, just cut back faded flower stalks in autumn after new flowering stems cease to appear. Clumps usually become overcrowded every 3 or 4 years; when this

(Continued on page 31)

Canna 'Cleopatra'

Clivia miniata

Chionodoxa luciliae

Caladium hortulanum

Camassia cusickii

happens, dig in early spring and cut rhizomes apart. Let cuts dry and heal over (about 24 hours), then replant in newly enriched soil.

In regions where winter temperatures fall below 0°F/−18°C, dig cannas after the first hard frost kills foliage. Cut off stems, knock soil from rhizomes, and let them dry for several days in a cool spot. Store over winter as for *Begonia*.

Container culture. Displayed in large pots or wooden planters, the shorter cannas are effective summer patio and terrace decorations. Follow directions "C" on page 91.

CHIONODOXA

GLORY-OF-THE-SNOW

Photo on page 30

Type of bulb: True bulb
Season of bloom: Late winter, early spring
Colors: Blue, white, pink
Grows to: 6 inches
When to plant: Autumn
Where to plant: Sun; where summers are hot, sun during bloom time, light shade thereafter
How deep to plant: 2 to 3 inches
Hardiness: To about −40°F/−40°C; needs some subfreezing winter temperatures

In their native lands, these charming small plants begin flowering as the snow melts at winter's end. Each bulb produces a stem to 6 inches tall; blossoms, shaped like six-pointed stars about an inch across, are spaced along the upper part of the stem. Leaves are straight and narrow, slightly shorter than the stem.

C. luciliae is the most frequently grown species. Each 6-inch stem carries about 10 bright blue blossoms with white centers. *C. l.* 'Alba' is pure white and a bit larger flowered; 'Gigantea' has larger leaves and larger blossoms of violet blue, while 'Rosea' is pink. *C. sardensis* produces blooms of deep gentian blue, each centered with a tiny white eye.

Uses. Naturalized under deciduous shrubs, glory-of-the-snow will in time create a carpet of flowers. It's also good in rock gardens and pathway border plantings.

Garden culture. In cool and mild-summer climates, choose a planting area in full sun. But where summers are hot, be sure the growing area is lightly shaded after bloom time.

Plant bulbs 2 to 3 inches deep, 3 inches apart, in well-drained soil enriched with organic matter before planting. Water regularly throughout the growing and blooming season; taper off when foliage begins to die back.

Bulbs increase rapidly and may be dug and separated for increase in early autumn, whenever plantings decline in vigor and bloom quality. (Plantings often increase from self-sown seedlings, as well.)

CLIVIA miniata

KAFFIR LILY

Photo on page 30

Type of bulb: Tuberous root
Season of bloom: Winter, spring
Colors: Yellow, orange, red
Grows to: 2 feet
When to plant: Any time of year (from containers); spring (from divisions)
Where to plant: Filtered sun or shade
How deep to plant: Juncture of leaf bases and roots at soil surface
Hardiness: To about 25°F/−4°C

Clivia is well described by the words "bold," "striking," and "colorful." Broad, strap-shaped leaves in lustrous dark green grow to about 1½ feet long, arching outward to form fountainlike clumps. Thick stems up to 2 feet tall rise from among the leaves, each crowned by a cluster of funnel-shaped 2-inch blossoms. Flowers are typically orange with yellow centers—but with a bit of nursery searching, you may find hybrids with blooms in yellow, soft orange, or red. Decorative red berries develop after the flowers fade.

Uses. The beauty of both foliage and flowers makes *Clivia* a good year-round accent plant for patio or shady garden—in a single clump or a mass planting, in containers or in the ground.

Garden culture. Where winters are frost free (or nearly so), plant *Clivia* in filtered sunlight to shade. Dig a liberal amount of organic matter into the soil before planting; set plants 1½ to 2 feet apart. (*Clivia* is sold only in containers.) Water regularly from winter through summer; cut back on water when growth slows in autumn, but never let leaves wilt.

Plants won't need dividing for many years after planting. When clumps do become overcrowded, dig and reset in spring, after flowering has ended.

Container culture. In most areas, container culture is the easiest way to meet *Clivia*'s needs. Follow directions "C" on page 91. Give monthly applications of a liquid fertilizer during spring and summer to enhance the next season's flowering.

Where winters are too cold for outdoor survival, container-grown clivias can spend winter inside in a brightly lit, cool room (night temperatures from 50° to 55°F/10° to 13°C).

Clivia blooms best when rootbound, so repot (in spring) only when plants look as if they're about to burst out of the container.

COLCHICUM

MEADOW SAFFRON

Photo on page 35

Type of bulb: Corm
Season of bloom: Late summer, early autumn; spring for *C. luteum* only
Colors: Lavender, violet, pink, white, yellow
Grows to: 6 to 8 inches
When to plant: Summer
Where to plant: Sun
How deep to plant: 3 inches
Hardiness: To about −30°F/−35°C

(Continued on next page)

Meadow saffron's delicate flowers rise from bare earth in late summer to early autumn, holding the stage without accompaniment of foliage. Blooms may be chalice shaped or starlike; each has six pointed petals atop a slim tube that acts as a stem. After the flowers wither, plants essentially vanish until the leaves emerge in spring. Leaves are straplike and up to a foot long; they aren't especially decorative, but last for just a few months and die back well in advance of the blooming season.

Bulb specialists may offer a number of *Colchicum* species, but at most nurseries you'll find only *C. autumnale* (often referred to as "autumn crocus") and several named hybrids. *C. autumnale*'s blossoms are about 2 inches wide; the usual color is pinkish lavender, though there's a white-flowered type as well. Available hybrids include 'The Giant' (lilac with white) and 'Waterlily' (double violet blooms). The oddity among colchicums is yellow-flowered, spring-blooming *C. luteum.*

Uses. Meadow saffron looks its best when naturalized along paths or walkways. Plant where flowers won't be obscured by taller plants, but where floppy leaves won't be too obtrusive.

Garden culture. Colchicums aren't fussy about soil type, but they do need good drainage. Plant corms in summer, setting them 6 to 8 inches apart and 3 inches deep. Be sure to provide some moisture throughout the year: water regularly in spring while plants are in leaf, then more sparingly during the brief midsummer dormant period—but not so sparsely that soil dries out completely. Resume regular watering when flowers appear.

Plantings may become overcrowded every 3 or 4 years. Dig and divide in midsummer as necessary.

Container culture. These accommodating plants will flower even without benefit of a container: dormant corms placed on a sunny (but not hot) window sill will bloom at the usual time. For basic container culture—with soil—see directions "B" on page 91.

COLOCASIA esculenta

ELEPHANT'S EAR
TARO
Photo on page 35

Type of bulb: Tuber
Season of bloom: Spring through autumn foliage; blooms unimportant
Color: Green foliage
Grows to: 6 feet
When to plant: Early spring
Where to plant: Light shade or filtered sun; sun where summers are cool
How deep to plant: 2 inches
Hardiness: Tops freeze at 30°F/−1°C; tubers survive to somewhat lower air temperatures, but die if soil freezes. In regions too cold for outdoor survival, dig and store over winter as for *Begonia*

The common name "elephant's ear" provides a good description of *Colocasia*'s enormous (to 2½ by 3 feet) heart-shaped leaves. Leathery to almost rubbery in texture, they're carried aloft at the ends of succulent stalks; an established clump of multiple tubers produces a display that can only be called junglelike. Inconspicuous flowers resemble greenish calla lilies (*Zantedeschia*); they appear only in the most temperate climates.

Uses. Elephant's ear is a peerless accent plant for creating tropical effects in light shade.

Garden culture. In all but cool-summer regions, where *Colocasia* can take full sun, choose a location in light shade or filtered sunlight. Rich soil and plenty of moisture produce the most impressive leaves, but good drainage isn't a requirement—plants grow in soggy soil, even in standing water.

Where winters are frost free, plant tubers in late winter or very early spring; elsewhere, wait until after the last-frost date. Enrich soil with organic matter before planting; then set out tubers 1 to 1½ feet apart and about 2 inches deep. Water frequently during the growing season;

fertilize monthly. When clumps become overcrowded, dig and divide in early spring.

In regions too cold for *Colocasia* to survive the winter outdoors, dig tubers after foliage is killed by frost and store over winter as for *Begonia.*

Container culture. In a suitably large container, elephant's ear is a spectacular summertime ornament for patio or terrace. Start tubers indoors (see *Begonia*) a month to 6 weeks before the expected late-frost date. Transplant to a container after the last frost, following directions "C" on page 91. Fertilize bimonthly with a high-nitrogen liquid fertilizer such as fish emulsion.

CONVALLARIA majalis

LILY-OF-THE-VALLEY
Photo on page 35

Type of bulb: Rhizome
Season of bloom: Spring
Colors: White, light pink
Grows to: 6 to 10 inches
When to plant: Autumn
Where to plant: Light shade or filtered sun
How deep to plant: 1 to 2 inches
Hardiness: To about −40°F/−40°C; needs some subfreezing winter temperatures

Lily-of-the-valley is justifiably a sentimental favorite in regions where there's enough winter chill for plants to prosper. Highly fragrant, delicate flowers account for part of the popularity; good-looking foliage throughout the growing season is a further asset.

Each rhizome (called a "pip") produces one slim flowering stem and two or three broad, lance-shaped leaves up to 9 inches long. Along the length of the stem, 12 to 20 small, waxy white bells hang from threadlike stalks. Bulb specialists occasionally offer a form with double white blossoms, as well as one with light pink bells.

Uses. Lily-of-the-valley makes a long-lived ground cover beneath deciduous shrubs and among other plants that need the same conditions.

Garden culture. Choose a garden location that's lightly shaded (or receives only filtered sunlight) and has good soil. Dig a generous quantity of organic matter into the soil before planting; then set out pips in clumps or drifts, 1 to 2 inches deep and 4 to 6 inches apart. Water plants regularly throughout the year (even during dormancy). Every year before new growth emerges, give planting a top dressing of compost, leaf mold, peat moss, or ground bark.

Divide plantings infrequently—only when performance starts to decline. Dig and separate rhizomes when leaves yellow in autumn.

Container culture. A potful of flowering lily-of-the-valley can be a charming patio decoration. Flowering plants can even be kept indoors as long as they're given bright indirect light (not direct sun) and fairly cool temperatures. Follow directions "B" on page 91.

CRINUM
Photo on page 35

Type of bulb: True bulb
Season of bloom: Late spring, summer
Colors: Pink, white
Grows to: 2 to 4 feet
When to plant: Any time of year, but autumn and early spring are best
Where to plant: Sun; filtered sun or part shade where summers are hot
How deep to plant: Top of bulb neck even with soil surface
Hardiness: To about 20°F/−7°C; in colder regions, grow as a container plant

Lush foliage and lilylike flowers of impressive size put *Crinum* high on the list of garden attention-getters. Each bulb tapers to an elongated stemlike neck from which radiate long, broad, strap-shaped leaves. In late spring through summer—the exact time depending on the species or hybrid—thick stems up to 4 feet

tall rise from the foliage, each bearing a cluster of long-stalked flowers. The blossoms resemble those of *Amaryllis*, but they're twice as big and open out a bit wider. Most are highly fragrant; colors include white and many shades of pink, from light to dark.

Though bulb specialists may offer a number of species and named hybrids, only a few types are available from the general nursery trade. *C. moorei* is one of the better known species; it has bright green, wavy-edged leaves and pinkish red blossoms to 4 inches or more across. You may also be able to find forms with white or soft pink flowers. *C. bulbispermum* has the same general appearance as *C. moorei*, but it's somewhat smaller in all parts and has narrower leaves. The typical flower color is white flushed with red on the outsides of petals, but pure white and pink forms also exist. *C. powellii*, a hybrid of these two species, produces clusters of pink or white 3-inch-wide blossoms on stems about 2 feet high.

Another hybrid occasionally offered by specialists is autumn-blooming *Amarcrinum memoria-corsii*, a cross between *Amaryllis belladonna* and *C. moorei*. *Amarcrinum* resembles *Crinum* in growth habit and foliage; its flowers look more like those of *Amaryllis*, having a narrower funnel shape than blooms of most crinums.

Uses. Crinums make attractive semipermanent accents among shrubs, perennials, and annuals.

Garden culture. Though you can plant bulbs at any time of year, early spring and autumn are preferred. Choose a full-sun location where summers are mild; in hot-summer climates, find a spot in filtered sun or one that receives midday or afternoon shade. Soil need not be especially well drained, but it should be liberally amended with organic matter prior to planting. Set in bulbs 2 to 4 feet apart, with tops of bulb necks even with the soil surface. Plants are somewhat drought tolerant—but for best performance, give regular to copious watering.

Divide crinums infrequently: the larger the clump becomes, the

more impressive its display of foliage and flowers. Protect foliage from slugs and snails.

Container culture. Follow directions "C" on page 91, choosing a container large enough to be in proportion to a full-grown plant. Where winter temperatures fall below 20°F/−7°C, overwinter plants indoors in a bright, cool room (night temperatures from 50° to 55°F/10° to 13°C).

CROCOSMIA
MONTBRETIA
Photo on page 35

Type of bulb: Corm
Season of bloom: Summer
Colors: Red, orange, bronze, yellow
Grows to: 2½ to 4 feet
When to plant: Spring
Where to plant: Sun; part shade where summers are hot
How deep to plant: 2 inches
Hardiness: To about 10°F/−12°C; to about −5°F/−21°C with winter protection (see page 89); in colder regions, dig and store over winter as for *Begonia*

These South African natives clearly show their relationship to *Gladiolus*, *Freesia*, *Ixia*, and *Sparaxis*. Foliage resembles that of *Gladiolus*, with sword-shaped leaves growing in upright fans. In *C. crocosmiiflora* (formerly *Tritonia crocosmiiflora* and commonly called "montbretia"), leaves may reach a height of 3 feet; the upright, branching stems grow in zigzag fashion to 3 to 4 feet. Each branch bears flat sprays of *Ixia*-like blossoms. The typical color is orange-scarlet, but with some nursery searching, you may be able to locate named varieties with blooms in hues ranging from yellow to orange and red to bronze.

C. masoniorum has shorter (to 2½ feet) and broader leaves than *C. crocosmiiflora*; its 2½ to 3-foot flower stems bend at nearly a right angle, much like the stems of some *Freesias*. A double row of 1½-inch orange to scarlet blossoms is borne on the horizontal part of each stem.

(Continued on next page)

Uses. *Crocosmia* looks attractive naturalized on sloping ground or set out to provide drifts of color among other plants. Single clumps can also be used effectively as accents in mixed plantings.

Garden culture. In cool and mild-summer regions, give *Crocosmia* full sun; where summers are hot, plants need some afternoon shade. Set out clumps of corms in well-drained soil enriched with organic matter, planting them about 2 inches deep and 3 inches apart. Once clumps are established, they'll perform with negligent watering—but for best results, water regularly throughout the growing and blooming period.

Where winter temperatures remain above 10°F/−12°C, corms are hardy in the ground; where lows fall between 10°F/−12°C and −5°F/−21°C, protect plantings with a mulch of straw or evergreen boughs. In colder regions, dig corms in early autumn after foliage yellows, dry them, and store as for *Begonia*.

Plantings increase in beauty as clumps grow thicker and larger, so divide and replant only when bulb's vigor and flower quality begin to deteriorate.

CROCUS

Photo on page 9

Type of bulb: Corm

Season of bloom: Autumn, winter, early spring

Colors: Lavender, purple, blue, yellow, orange, cream, white, bicolors

Grows to: 6 inches

When to plant: Autumn

Where to plant: Sun; filtered sun where summers are hot

How deep to plant: 2 to 3 inches

Hardiness: To about −40°F/−40°C; most need some subfreezing winter temperatures

If you live in a climate where crocuses grow well, you can enjoy a 7-month-long blooming season. Autumn-flowering species may come into bloom as early as late Au-

gust; winter-blooming types will carry on where the climate allows. And as their season draws to a close, the many late winter and early spring species and hybrids take the stage.

All crocuses have rather grass-like leaves, often with a silvery midrib. In the autumn-flowering group, flowers appear before foliage; the rest develop leaves before or during flowering. The flower tube flares at the top into a six-segmented blossom, usually a chalice shaped. Blooms appear stemless, since the short true stems are hidden underground.

Nurseries usually offer a selection of Dutch crocus hybrids derived from *C. vernus.* They may also stock a few of the species, but a bulb specialist will have the greatest species selection. Though species crocuses usually have smaller blooms than the Dutch hybrids, they often produce more flowers from each corm. Here are a few of the more widely available species:

• *C. speciosus.* The best known and showiest of autumn-flowering species. Large blue violet flowers have brilliant orange stigmas. Named varieties are available in pale and dark blue, lavender, and white; flower segments may be as long as 3 inches.

• *C. kotschyanus* (formerly *C. zonatus*). September-blooming; delicate pinkish lavender or lilac flowers with white stamens.

• *C. ancyrensis.* Orange yellow; the earliest spring crocus.

• *C. chrysanthus.* Sweet-scented orange yellow flowers have black-tipped anthers.

• *C. sieberi.* Delicate lavender blue flowers with golden throats. In the Northeast, this species blooms as soon as the snow melts.

• *C. susianus* (cloth-of-gold crocus). Brilliant orange-gold, starlike flowers; each segment has a dark brown stripe down the center. Blooms in January or February in the West, March in the Midwest and East.

• *C. tomasinianus.* One of the most easily grown species, with slender buds and star-shaped flowers of silvery lavender blue. Tips of segments may be marked with a dark blotch. Extremely prolific when well estab-

lished, covering the ground with bloom in late January or early February in more moderate climates, March in colder areas.

Uses. For patches and drifts of color at ground level, crocuses are unexcelled. Plant corms in dappled shade beneath deciduous trees and shrubs, or naturalize them in grassy areas that can remain unmowed until crocus foliage ripens. Just a few corms can create small, jewel-like patches of color in rock gardens, between paving stones, in rock walls, and in gravel pathways.

Garden culture. Crocuses are not particular about soil type, but they do require good drainage. They prefer a sunny location except in hot-summer areas, where filtered sun is best. Plant corms as soon as they're available in autumn; set them 2 to 3 inches deep, 3 to 4 inches apart. Give regular watering during the growth and flowering period; taper off when foliage begins to yellow. Crocuses prefer a dry dormant period, but will also accept watering during that time if soil is well drained.

Crocus corms increase rapidly and will be ready for dividing after 3 to 4 years.

Container culture. Follow basic directions "B" on page 91. You also can force crocuses for earlier bloom according to methods outlined on pages 92 and 93.

CYCLAMEN

Photo on page 38

Type of bulb: Tuber

Season of bloom: Autumn, winter, spring, summer

Colors: Purple, lavender, pink, red, white

Grows to: 1 foot

When to plant: Summer or early autumn

Where to plant: Filtered sun or light shade

How deep to plant: ½ inch (except for *C. persicum;* see below)

Hardiness: To about 0°F/−18°C; to about 25°F/−4°C for *C. persicum*

(Continued on page 36)

Crocosmia crocosmiiflora

Convallaria majalis

Crinum powellii

Colocasia esculenta

Colchicum autumnale

The large-flowered florists' cyclamen (*C. persicum*) is familiar to gardeners and nongardeners alike as a container-grown gift plant, often sold during the winter holiday season. Not as widely known, but much more successfully adapted to outdoor culture in many regions, are the various smaller *Cyclamen* species.

All cyclamens have flowers resembling those of the perennial shooting star (*Dodecatheon*): elongated, somewhat twisted petals flare back sharply from a central ring that's often darker than the petals (or in a contrasting hue). Leaves are heart shaped to rounded, each carried at the end of a long, fleshy stalk. In many species, foliage is marbled or patterned in silvery white or light green—beautiful in its own right. Most cyclamens go through a leafless or near leafless dormant period at some time during summer.

C. persicum, the florists' cyclamen, is the largest (to 1 foot tall) and showiest of the group, available in the greatest color range: lavender, purple, red shades, pink shades, and white. Bloom begins in late autumn and continues until early spring. Leaves may be solid green or patterned in light green or silver.

Though *C. persicum* can endure a bit of frost—to about 25°F/−4°C—it's usually grown as a container plant, spending its winter bloom period indoors in a bright, cool room.

The "hardy" species of *Cyclamen,* smaller than *C. persicum,* will take winter temperatures down to 0°F/−18°C. Two easy-to-grow members of this group are widely available. *C. hederifolium* (*C. neapolitanum*) blooms in late summer or early autumn; its rose pink or white flowers, borne on 4 to 6-inch stems, appear before the leaves. The ivylike foliage—light green marbled with silver and white—is especially handsome. *C. coum* and its numerous subspecies begin flowering with the new year and continue to bloom until earliest spring. A typical plant has solid green leaves and rosy crimson flowers on 4 to 6-inch stems, but pink and white-blossomed forms and subspecies are also sold, some with silver-patterned foliage.

With a little nursery searching, you may also be able to find several other hardy cyclamens. Spring-blooming *C. repandum* has narrow-petaled crimson flowers on 6-inch stems; its ivylike, tooth-edged leaves are marbled with silver. The same description nearly covers midsummer-blooming *C. purpurascens* (*C. europaeum*), but its blossoms are fragrant and its red-backed leaves are nearly evergreen. *C. cilicium* blooms from early autumn into midwinter; its pale pink flowers (or white, in the case of *C. c.* 'Album') are carried on 3 to 6-inch stems. Leaves are marked with silver and appear very early in the blooming season.

Uses. The hardy cyclamens are fine "woodland wildflower" plants for locations in light shade or filtered sun. Plant them in small groups or large drifts, or even as a ground cover beneath trees or shrubs.

In regions where outdoor culture is possible, florists' cyclamen can be used as a bedding plant along pathway borders and in the foreground of lightly shaded gardens. In pots or planters, it adds winter color to patios and decks.

Garden culture. Hardy cyclamens need well-drained soil liberally amended with organic matter prior to planting. Space tubers 6 to 12 inches apart, covering them with ½ inch of soil. Plants need moisture throughout the year, so be sure to water regularly during rainless periods. Each year, just after flowers finish, topdress the soil with about ½ inch of leaf mold or compost; this will provide enough nutrition for continued good performance the following year and keep soil in top condition for plants' shallow roots.

Tubers grow a bit larger each year, producing more and more flowers and leaves as time goes on. They do not produce increases, but can multiply by self-sown seeds. If you need to transplant a cyclamen, do so during the tuber's brief summer dormant period.

In mild-winter regions (temperatures no lower than 25°F/−4°C), *C. persicum* can be grown outdoors in the same manner as the hardy species. Don't cover tubers with soil, though: plant so that the upper one-third to one-half is above the soil surface.

Container culture. For florists' cyclamen, use one of the soil mixes described under "B" on page 91. Plant each tuber in a pot big enough to leave 2 inches of soil between all sides of the tuber and the container edges. Plant tubers so the top one-third to one-half is above the soil surface.

During the growing and blooming season, water plants regularly, but never let the container sit in a saucer of water. Once a month, apply a liquid fertilizer diluted to half strength. When you take plants indoors to escape freezing weather, give them a well-lit location (in a north or east-facing window, for example) in a cool room—ideally about 50°F/10°C at night, no warmer than 65°F/18°C during the daytime.

Plants go nearly dormant in summer; at that time, place containers in a cool, shaded spot and water infrequently. When growth resumes in late summer or early autumn, repot tubers in fresh soil and begin regular watering.

DAHLIA

Photos on pages 19 and 38

Type of bulb: Tuberous root

Season of bloom: Summer, early autumn

Colors: Every color but blue and true green; many multicolors

Grows to: 1 to 7 feet

When to plant: Spring

Where to plant: Sun; part shade where summers are hot

How deep to plant: 3 inches initially (see below)

Hardiness: To about 20°F/−7°C; in colder regions, dig and store over winter (see below)

Dahlias are one of the most varied and variable of the summer-flowering bulbous plants. They grow from 1 foot to over 7 feet tall, bearing flowers that range from about 2 inches to a foot in diameter. Colors include every hue but blue and spectrum green, and many varieties are patterned or shaded with a second color. And though they're native to Mexico, dahlias are amazingly adaptable: they grow from coast to coast and in a great latitudinal range, encompassing both short and long-summer climates.

The American Dahlia Society has established a certain order in these plants' great diversity by dividing flower types into 12 groups, each including plants of varying heights. Specialists use these classifications in describing available varieties, though the general nursery trade may not.

Uses. Plant dahlias in separate flower beds or in combination with other plants. Use smaller types as border hedges or short accents, taller ones as background screen or hedge plants or for striking accents.

Garden culture. Plant dahlias in spring, after air and soil temperatures have warmed. The easiest gauge to planting time is this: when the time is right for tomatoes, corn, and potatoes, it's right for dahlias as well. Choose a location in full sun except where summers are hot and dry; in these areas, plants need shade during the hottest part of the day. Also keep in mind that flowers face the source of light; select the planting area accordingly.

Dahlias grow best in well-drained soil liberally enriched with organic matter. Space roots of larger dahlias (over 4 feet tall) 4 to 5 feet apart, roots of smaller types 1 to 2 feet apart. For each root, dig a 1-foot-deep planting hole—about 1½ feet across for larger dahlias, 9 to 12 inches across for smaller ones. Incorporate about ¼ cup of granular low-nitrogen fertilizer into the soil at the bottom of the hole; then add 4 inches of pulverized soil if the native soil is on the sandy side, about 6 inches if it's more claylike.

If you're planting a tall variety, drive a 5 to 6-foot stake into the hole just off center; then place the root horizontally in the bottom of the hole, 2 inches from the stake and with the growth eye pointing toward it. (No stake is needed for shorter dahlias.) Cover the root with 3 inches of soil, then water thoroughly. Unless weather is dry and soil loses its moisture, don't water again until growth begins.

As the shoots grow, gradually fill in the hole with soil. For tall-growing varieties, thin out shoots when they're about 6 inches tall, leaving only the strongest one or two. When these shoots have three pairs of leaves, pinch out the growing tip just above the upper set of leaves to encourage bushy growth. Varieties with small flowers need just one pinching, but if you're growing large-flowered dahlias, pinch again after subsequent growth has produced three pairs of leaves.

Dahlias grow rapidly, so they need a steady supply of water after shoots emerge. Each time you water, be sure to moisten the soil to a depth of at least 1 foot. Mulch soil to conserve moisture.

Well-prepared soil should contain enough nutrients to last plants through the season. But if your soil is light or if roots remained in the ground the previous year, apply a granular low-nitrogen fertilizer when the first flower buds show. During the growing and blooming period, watch for mildew on foliage.

In autumn, after plants turn yellow or have been frosted (whichever comes first), cut stalks to within 6 inches of the ground. Where winter temperatures remain above 20°F/ −7°C, you can leave roots undisturbed through a second and sometimes even a third bloom season before you dig and separate. But most growers, even those living in such mild-weather regions, prefer to dig annually. Carefully dig a 2-foot-diameter circle around each plant and gently pry up the clump with a spading fork. Shake off loose soil, being careful not to break roots apart; then let the clump dry in the sun for several hours.

At this point, you have two choices: you can divide roots immediately, or store clumps intact and divide them several weeks before planting in spring. Autumn division is simpler, since you can easily recognize growth eyes and the separated roots are easier to store. However, autumn-separated roots are more likely to shrivel in storage, and are also more susceptible to rot. To divide clumps, cut them apart with a sharp knife, making sure that each separate root is attached to a portion of stalk with a visible growth eye (see page 89).

If you divide in autumn, dust each cut with sulfur to prevent rot during storage. Several weeks before planting time, place roots in moist sand to plump them up and encourage sprouting.

If you divide in spring, do so 2 to 4 weeks prior to planting, then plump up roots in moist sand.

To store divided roots or clumps over winter, place them in a single layer and cover with dry sand, sawdust, peat moss, vermiculite, or perlite. Keep in a dark, dry, cool place (40° to 45°F/4° to 7°C) until spring. Check occasionally for signs of shriveling; lightly moisten the storage material if necessary.

DIETES

AFRICAN IRIS
FORTNIGHT LILY

Photo on page 38

Type of bulb: Rhizome
Season of bloom: Possible all year
Colors: White, light yellow
Grows to: 1½ to 3 feet
When to plant: Any time of year (from containers); autumn or winter (from divisions)
Where to plant: Sun or light shade
How deep to plant: Top of rhizome just beneath soil surface
Hardiness: To about 15°F/−9°C

Both in foliage and blossom, the *Dietes* species and varieties are very irislike. The narrow, flat, evergreen leaves are arranged in fans; the branching stems carry flattish, six-segmented blossoms that could pass for beardless irises. Though each flower lasts only one day, each blossom stalk carries a seemingly inexhaustible supply of buds. Flowering comes in bursts throughout spring, summer, and autumn—and even in winter, in very mild climates.

For many years these plants were grouped with *Moraea* and some nurseries still offer them under the old names. *D. vegeta* (formerly known as *D. iridioides* or *Moraea iridioides*) is the most widely grown species. It's also one of the largest flowered and tallest (2 to 3 feet);

(Continued on page 39)

Endymion hispanicus

Dahlia *hybrid*

Cyclamen persicum

Eremurus *hybrid*

Dietes vegeta

both stems and foliage are evergreen. The 3-inch, waxy white blossoms are decorated on their three outer segments with an orange-and-brown blotch and some blue shading. Variety 'Johnsonii' is larger and more robust.

D. bicolor's flowers, light yellow with dark brown blotches, are slightly smaller and more rounded than those of D. vegeta. They're carried on 2 to 3-foot flower stems, each of which lasts just one year.

Two white-flowered hybrids of these species are occasionally sold. 'Orange Drops' has an orange spot on three of the six flower segments; 'Lemon Drops' has yellow spots. Both hybrids resemble D. vegeta in stem and foliage size, but have smaller, rounder blossoms more like those of D. bicolor.

Foliage and height distinguish the plant sold as D. catenulata from the preceding group. Its leaves are broader and grow to about 1½ feet; the branching stems carry white blossoms similar to and slightly smaller than those of D. vegeta.

Uses. This plant's thick clumps of narrow leaves are good looking all year. Use it as a garden accent; it's especially effective in Japanese gardens and near water or rocks.

Garden culture. All Dietes species and hybrids look their best when grown in good soil and watered regularly. But one of their virtues is toughness: once established, they'll give a satisfactory performance even in poor soil and with infrequent or erratic watering. Select a sunny or lightly shaded planting area; then set out nursery plants about 2 feet apart, keeping tops of rhizomes even with the soil surface. (Dietes is sold only in containers—bare rhizomes are not available.)

Clumps may remain undisturbed for many years. If you need to divide or move them, do so in autumn or winter.

Container culture. The smaller D. catenulata can be a conversation-piece hanging basket plant; plantlets will droop from its arching stems in the fashion of spider plant (Chlorophytum). Follow directions "C" on page 91.

ENDYMION

BLUEBELL
Photo on page 38

Type of bulb: True bulb
Season of bloom: Spring
Colors: Blue, white, pink
Grows to: 12 to 20 inches
When to plant: Autumn
Where to plant: Light shade or filtered sun
How deep to plant: 3 inches
Hardiness: To about −30°F/−35°C

Both Spanish bluebell (E. hispanicus, formerly Scilla campanulata, S. hispanica) and English bluebell (E. non-scriptus, formerly Scilla non-scripta) are trouble-free bulbs. Spanish bluebell is the taller of the two, with straplike leaves and erect flower stems up to 20 inches tall. Twelve or more ¾-inch bell-shaped flowers hang from each stem's upper length. English bluebell's flower stalks reach only about 1 foot and are gently arching rather than upright; the fragrant blossoms are slightly smaller and narrower than those of Spanish bluebell. Both species are available in blue, white, and pink forms.

Uses. Easy-care bluebell is for drift plantings or for naturalizing at the edges of woodland areas.

Garden culture. The type of bluebell that's best for your garden depends on climate. English bluebell prefers definite winter cold and moderate to cool summer weather; it's generally unsuccessful where summers are hot and winters mild. Spanish bluebell, on the other hand, thrives in warmer areas and can even spread by self-sown seedlings.

Choose a location in light shade or filtered sunlight. Set bulbs out in clumps or drifts, planting them about 3 inches deep and 6 inches apart; water regularly from planting time until foliage dies. Divide infrequently; display increases in beauty as plantings increase.

Container culture. Follow directions "B" on page 91.

ERANTHIS hyemalis

WINTER ACONITE
Photo on page 15

Type of bulb: Tuber
Season of bloom: Late winter, very early spring
Color: Yellow
Grows to: 2 to 8 inches
When to plant: Late summer, as soon as available
Where to plant: Sun during bloom time, part shade during rest of year
How deep to plant: 3 inches
Hardiness: To about −10°F/−23°C; needs some subfreezing winter temperatures

Winter aconite is one of the harbingers of spring: blossoming stems often come up through snow, appearing before the leaves. Each stem bears its 1½-inch, buttercuplike yellow flower on a leafy collar. The basal leaves (emerging later on) are rounded and divided into narrow lobes.

Uses. Rock gardens, pathway borders, and woodland plantings are all good settings for winter aconite. For an attractive mixed planting, combine it with other bulbs blooming at the same time: Iris reticulata, snowdrop (Galanthus), and Siberian squill (Scilla siberica).

Garden culture. The best planting location for winter aconite is one that receives full sun during bloom time, part shade during the rest of the year.

Purchase and plant tubers in late summer, as soon as they're available in nurseries; if they look dry or shriveled, plump them up in wet sand before planting. Set them about 3 inches deep and 4 inches apart in good, well-drained soil enriched with organic matter before planting.

Throughout the growing and blooming season, keep soil moist (but not saturated).

Divide plants infrequently; it takes them a year or more to re-establish. Separate into small clumps rather than individual tubers.

EREMURUS

FOXTAIL LILY

Photo on page 38

Type of bulb: Tuberous root
Season of bloom: Spring
Colors: White, cream, buff, yellow, orange, pink
Grows to: 4 to 9 feet
When to plant: Autumn
Where to plant: Sun
How deep to plant: 1 inch
Hardiness: To about −20°F/−29°C; needs some subfreezing winter temperatures

Foxtail lily's height is impressive: flowering stems grow from 4 to 9 feet tall, rising from fountainlike rosettes of narrow, strap-shaped leaves. The upper third to half of each stem is packed with ½ to 1-inch-wide starlike blossoms; buds open in sequence from the bottom, giving the half-open spike the look of a fox's tail.

Pink-flowered *E. robustus* easily attains 8 to 9 feet, and white-flowered *E. himalaicus* is only 1 to 2 feet shorter. The Shelford Hybrids reach 4 to 5 feet, bearing blooms in pink, yellow, buff, orange, or white. Foliage dies down after bloom; new leaves don't emerge until early the next spring.

Uses. These stately plants add vertical accents to the late spring garden.

Garden culture. Choose a sunny location and good, well-drained soil enriched with organic matter. Plant 2 to 4 feet apart. Dig a hole large enough to accommodate roots easily; spread them at about a 45-degree angle and cover with soil so the growing point is 1 inch below the surface. Handle roots carefully; they're brittle and may rot if damaged.

Water regularly from the onset of growth until foliage has died back; water less frequently throughout late summer and autumn.

New growth can be harmed by freezing nights. To prevent damage, give winter protection (see page 89); remove after danger of hard frosts is past.

ERYTHRONIUM

ADDER'S TONGUE
DOG-TOOTH VIOLET
FAWN LILY
TROUT LILY

Photo on page 43

Type of bulb: Corm
Season of bloom: Spring
Colors: Purple, pink, lavender, yellow, cream, white
Grows to: 6 to 18 inches
When to plant: Autumn
Where to plant: Filtered sunlight or light to moderate shade; part shade for *E. dens-canis*
How deep to plant: 2 to 3 inches
Hardiness: To about −40°F/−40°C; needs some subfreezing winter temperatures

Most species of *Erythronium* are woodland plants with lilylike flowers and broad, tongue-shaped, brown-mottled leaves. Because these plants are fairly exacting in their cultural requirements, they're generally sold only by bulb specialists—particularly those in the western United States, where a number of species are native.

The various species have accumulated a number of common names, most describing the shape or mottling of the foliage. *E. americanum*, one of several species from eastern North America, is called trout lily or adder's tongue—the first name referring to the mottling on the leaves, the second to their shape. Each 6-inch leaf is splotched with purplish brown and near white; one nodding, yellow, 2-inch flower tops each 9 to 12-inch stem.

Brown-mottled 6-inch leaves give the name fawn lily to *E. californicum*; up to three yellow-based white or cream flowers are borne atop each 6 to 10-inch stem. *E. revolutum* is similar but taller (to 16 inches), larger, and lavender-flowered. 'Rose Beauty' and 'White Beauty' are selected varieties.

Dog-tooth violet, *E. dens-canis*, takes its name from the shape of its corm. The 4 to 6-inch leaves are mottled brown and white; a single 1-inch blossom appears on each 6 to 12-inch stem. The typical flower color is deep pink to purple, but specialists offer selections in white and other colors. *E. hendersonii*'s dark green, brown-mottled leaves may reach 8 inches long. Stems grow up to 1 foot tall, topped with one to four nodding lavender flowers.

Foot-long leaves of yellowish green distinguish *E. tuolumnense* from the above species. Each 12 to 15-inch stem supports several starlike yellow blossoms. 'Kondo' and 'Pagoda' are two vigorous selected forms, generally taller (to 1½ feet) and easier to grow than the species.

Uses. Plant clumps or drifts in woodland gardens, rock gardens, along pathways, or under deciduous trees and shrubs.

Garden culture. With the exception of *E. dens-canis*, which needs only partial shade (preferably during the hot afternoon hours), all species do best in filtered sunlight or light to moderate shade. Plant corms in clumps or drifts, 2 to 3 inches deep and 4 to 5 inches apart, in well-drained soil liberally amended with organic matter. Except for *E. californicum*, these plants need moisture the year around. Divide plantings infrequently—only when vigor and bloom quality decline.

EUCHARIS grandiflora

AMAZON LILY

Photo on page 43

Type of bulb: True bulb
Season of bloom: Primarily winter, but can bloom periodically throughout the year given the right culture and climate
Color: White
Grows to: 1½ to 2 feet
When to plant: Any time of year
Where to plant: Light shade
How deep to plant: Tip of bulb even with soil surface
Hardiness: Tender; store indoors over winter except as noted

Except in absolutely frost-free areas, Amazon lily is strictly a container plant, to be brought inside during the coldest part of the year (or kept indoors all year long). Its thin-textured, glossy, tongue-shaped leaves grow up to 1 foot long, supported by equally long leaf stalks. The 2-foot flowering stems support clusters of up to six fragrant white blossoms, each one resembling a 3-inch daffodil.

Uses. Good-looking foliage and flowers make *Eucharis* an ideal choice for a house plant, or for patio, deck, or terrace in warm weather.

Garden culture. To try Amazon lily in the garden, choose a spot where plants will receive as much light as possible without direct sun. Plant bulbs 4 inches apart, tips even with the soil surface, in well-drained soil liberally amended with organic matter. Water regularly. Crowded clumps give the best performance.

Container culture. Follow directions "C" on page 91. Water bulbs well just after potting, then water sparingly until growth begins. Increase water as leaves grow, keeping soil moist; every other week, apply liquid fertilizer at half strength.

After bloom finishes, stop fertilizing and cut back on water, giving just enough to keep leaves from wilting. When new growth begins, resume regular watering and fertilizing. Using this technique, you may get several flowerings in a year.

Repot or divide Amazon lily only when plants crowd their pot to capacity.

EUCOMIS

PINEAPPLE FLOWER
Photo on page 43

Type of bulb: True bulb
Season of bloom: Summer
Colors: Green with purple
Grows to: 2 to 3 feet
When to plant: Early autumn (in ground); spring (in containers)
Where to plant: Sun; filtered sun or light shade where summers are hot
How deep to plant: 4 to 6 inches
Hardiness: To about 5°F/ − 15°C

As its common name suggests, *Eucomis* presents a convincing imitation of a pineapple fruit: the upper portion of each flowering spike is surrounded by a tight cylindrical cluster of fragrant starlike blossoms and topped with a tuft of leafy bracts. Decorative purplish seed capsules follow the flowers.

E. bicolor has green blossoms with purple petal edges; flower spikes reach about 2 feet, rising from rosettes of broad, wavy-edged leaves. *E. comosa* (sometimes sold as *E. punctata*) grows up to 3 feet tall with leaves to 2 feet long; its greenish white blossoms are tinged with pink or purple.

Uses. *Eucomis* is a conversation piece when in bloom, and an attractive foliage plant at all times. Grow it in a container or at the foreground of garden plantings.

Garden culture. Choose a location in full sun (in filtered sun or light shade where summers are hot), and enrich the soil with organic matter. Then set bulbs 4 to 6 inches deep and 1 foot apart. When growth begins in spring, apply a granular fertilizer. Water regularly during the growing and blooming season, but give little or no water during winter dormancy—plants can usually survive on rainfall. Divide plants infrequently, perhaps every 5 or 6 years.

Container culture. Select a large, deep container and follow directions "C" on page 91; plant bulbs with tips just beneath the surface. For best results, repot yearly in fresh soil.

FREESIA

Photo on page 11

Type of bulb: Corm
Season of bloom: Early spring
Colors: Every color but true green
Grows to: 1 to 1½ feet
When to plant: Autumn
Where to plant: Sun or part shade
How deep to plant: 2 inches
Hardiness: To about 20°F/ − 7°C; in colder regions, grow in containers

To people who know them, freesias and fragrance are synonymous. In times past, the most widely available type was creamy white, powerfully sweet-scented *F. alba* (*F. refracta alba*); in favorable climates, it naturalizes easily. Today, the most popular freesias are newer hybrids that feature larger blossoms and a great range of colors.

All freesias have trumpet-shaped flowers, up to 2 inches long and flaring to 2 inches across. They're borne on wiry stems that rise 1 to 1½ feet tall. Each stem bends at nearly a right angle just beneath the lowest bud, so a double rank of blossoms faces upward (or nearly so). Narrow, swordlike leaves up to 1 foot tall grow in irislike fans.

Uses. Try naturalizing freesias in clumps or drifts, or use them in borders of drought-tolerant plants—including other summer-dormant bulbs.

Garden culture. For best performance, freesias require well-drained soil and little or no watering during summer. Group corms in clumps or drifts, planting them 2 inches deep and only about 2 inches apart. (Setting plants close together lets the somewhat floppy blooming stems hold each other up.) Water regularly throughout the growing and blooming season; cut back on water when foliage starts to yellow, and keep soil dry until new growth emerges in autumn.

Freesia corms increase rapidly. Dig and divide them for increase after several years, if you wish; or leave in place until vigor and bloom quality decline. Dig when foliage yellows, then store over summer as for *Gladiolus;* replant in early autumn.

Container culture. Plant corms 1 inch apart and 2 inches deep, following directions "B" on page 91. In cold-winter climates, you can grow freesias indoors in a cool room—40° to 50°F/4° to 10°C at night, up to 65°F/18°C in a sunny window during the day. Netherlands bulb growers produce cold-treated corms that can be potted in spring to bloom in summer the first year. In subsequent years, these will bloom at the normal time in early spring.

FRITILLARIA

FRITILLARY

Photo on page 43

Type of bulb: True bulb
Season of bloom: Spring
Colors: Red, orange, yellow, maroon, purple shades, cream, white
Grows to: 6 inches to 4 feet
When to plant: Autumn
Where to plant: Sun, filtered sun, or light shade, depending on type
How deep to plant: 3 to 5 inches, depending on type
Hardiness: Varies (see below); most need some subfreezing winter temperatures

The fritillaries are a contradictory group of plants. Most have a wildflower charm, though blossoms are often rather strangely and intricately marked. But the best known species would hardly fit anyone's idea of a woodland wildflower. *F. imperialis*, the crown imperial, is the exceptional individual. Its thick stems grow 3 to 4 feet tall, clothed for about half their height in whorls of lance-shaped 6-inch leaves. At the top of each stem is a circular cluster of drooping, bell-shaped flowers topped by a thick tuft of leaflike bracts. Blossoms are about 2 inches long; the usual color is red, but orange and yellow forms are also available. All types have a musky odor which some people find objectionable.

Toward the other end of the height scale is *F. meleagris*, commonly called checkered lily or snakeshead. Each slender stem reaches just 12 to 15 inches, rising above three or more narrow 3 to 6-inch leaves. The nodding, bell-shaped 2-inch blooms—carried one to three per stem—are typically marked in an unusual checkerboard pattern. The most common color combination is light with dark maroon, but numerous variations exist: pale gray with brownish purple, white with light violet, and solid colors of dark purple, lilac, and white.

From the western United States comes *F. lanceolata*, the checker lily. Its flowers, marked in a check-erboard design of brownish purple and yellow shades, are borne on stems to 2½ feet tall. Narrow leaves grow in whorls on the lower part of the stems. *F. recurva* (scarlet fritillary), another westerner, has the same general appearance as *F. lanceolata* and reaches about the same height. Its bell-shaped flowers are solid red centered with yellow. Three-foot-tall *F. persica* also has leaves that grow in whorls on the lower part of each stem. But its blossoms—drooping, plum colored bells—are carried in spikes covering the stem's top portion.

Bulb specialists may offer a number of other species in addition to those just mentioned. Most are similar in growth habit to one of the types described.

Uses. Naturalize fritillaries in grassland or meadow areas; smaller species are also attractive in rock gardens and at the margins of woodland plantings. Crown imperial makes a striking color accent in mixed perennial, bulb, and annual groupings.

Garden culture. All fritillaries appreciate some winter chilling and tend to perform poorly where summers are hot and dry. *F. imperialis* and *F. meleagris* are hardy to about −20°F/−29°C; other species can usually survive in the ground down to about −10°F/−23°C.

F. imperialis and *F. persica* can take full sun where summers are cool and overcast; elsewhere, plant them in a location receiving light shade during summer. The other fritillaries prefer filtered sunlight or light shade everywhere.

These plants need good, well-drained soil enriched with organic matter before planting. Set the large bulbs of *F. imperialis* 4 to 5 inches deep, 8 to 12 inches apart; plant the smaller species 3 to 4 inches deep, 6 inches apart. Give plants regular watering during the growth and flowering period; cut back on water as foliage dies back in summer. After foliage is gone, all but *F. meleagris* can go without water until autumn.

Established bulbs seldom need dividing; dig and separate only when you want to increase plantings.

GALANTHUS

SNOWDROP

Photo on page 9

Type of bulb: True bulb
Season of bloom: Late winter, early spring
Colors: White with green
Grows to: 6 to 12 inches
When to plant: Autumn; spring (from divisions)
Where to plant: Sun during bloom time, light shade during rest of year
How deep to plant: 3 to 4 inches
Hardiness: To about −40°F/−40°C; needs some subfreezing winter temperatures

In the cold-weather climates they prefer, snowdrops are often the first bulbs to bloom as winter draws to a close. Even if a snowfall catches plants in flower, the blossoming stems will pop back up again—as long as snow melts soon.

Several *Galanthus* species and varieties are sold. In all types, each stem bears one pendant, six-petaled flower; the three inner petals are always shorter than the three outer ones, and are usually marked or infused with green.

Though all snowdrops need a climate in which at least some winter night temperatures drop below 32°F/0°C, the giant snowdrop, *G. elwesii*, is adapted to regions without too much winter chill. Its flowers are rather egg-shaped and up to 1½ inches long; inner petals are heavily infused with green. Stems grow to 1 foot, rising above two or three narrow 8-inch leaves.

Common snowdrop, *G. nivalis*, grows 6 to 9 inches tall; it has inch-long bell-shaped flowers, the inner petals marked at the tips with a precise green crescent. Variety 'Flore Pleno' has double blooms.

Uses. Snowdrops find their niche in the winter woodland landscape, in rock gardens, and among plantings of deciduous shrubs or trees.

Garden culture. An ideal location for snowdrops is near deciduous trees or shrubs, so the planting area will be sunny during the bulbs'

(Continued on page 44)

Eucharis grandiflora

Fritillaria imperialis

Eucomis comosa

Erythronium californicum

flowering period, but lightly shaded later in the year. Enrich soil with organic matter; then set bulbs 3 to 4 inches deep and 3 inches apart. Snowdrops prefer moisture the year around; water periodically when rainfall isn't sufficient.

Snowdrop bulbs may stay in place for many years. If you need to divide or move plants, do so just after flowers fade. Try to keep plenty of soil around bulbs; replant immediately and water regularly.

GALTONIA candicans

SUMMER HYACINTH

Type of bulb: True bulb

Season of bloom: Summer

Color: White

Grows to: 2 to 4 feet

When to plant: Autumn; spring where winter temperatures fall below 10°F/−12°C

Where to plant: Sun; light shade where summers are hot

How deep to plant: 6 inches

Hardiness: To about 10°F/−12°C; to about −20°F/−29°C with winter protection (see page 89); in colder regions, dig and store over winter as for *Gladiolus*

Despite its common name, *Galtonia* doesn't look much like the familiar spring-blooming *Hyacinthus*. Each bulb produces a stout, erect stem that carries a spire of 20 or more pendant white blossoms; each fragrant, bell-shaped bloom is about 1½ inches long. The floppy, strap-shaped leaves reach a length of 2 to 3 feet.

Uses. Summer hyacinth's white-flowered spikes add height and a dash of coolness to the summer garden.

Garden culture. Summer hyacinth revels in rich soil and lots of water. Dig plenty of organic matter into the soil in advance of planting; choose a sunny spot if your summers are cool to moderate, a lightly shaded location in hot-summer regions. Plant bulbs 6 inches deep, 1 foot apart—

in autumn where winter lows won't fall below 10°F/−12°C, in spring in colder regions. Water plants regularly throughout the growth and flowering season, and protect them from slugs and snails.

Summer hyacinth gives the best display if allowed to remain undisturbed from one year to the next. Where winter low temperatures fall between 10°F/−12°C and −20°F/−29°C, protect the planting area with a winter mulch (see page 89) after foliage dies down. In colder regions, dig bulbs annually and store them over winter as for *Gladiolus*.

If you need to divide or move plantings, do so at the best planting time for your climate.

GLADIOLUS

Photo on page 46

Type of bulb: Corm

Season of bloom: Late spring, summer, autumn

Colors: Every color but true blue

Grows to: 1½ to 6 feet

When to plant: Autumn, winter, or spring (see below)

Where to plant: Sun

How deep to plant: 3 to 6 inches, depending on size of corm

Hardiness: To about 10°F/−12°C; in colder regions, dig and store over winter (see below)

At the mention of the word "gladiolus," most gardeners think of the magnificent, variously colored, large-flowered garden hybrids known to botanists as *G. hortulanus*. These types grow 3 to 6 feet tall, bearing blossoms up to 6 inches across. The funnel-shaped flowers, widely flaring and usually ruffled at the edges, all face in one direction; they're closely spaced on the flowering spike and arranged alternately on either side of it. Leaves are arranged in narrow, upright fans. They're shaped like swords, hence the plant's botanical name—*gladiolus* means "little sword" in Latin.

Less well known than *G. hortulanus*, but no less attractive, are the various species *Gladiolus*.

These are generally shorter than their large hybrid kin, with smaller blossoms and foliage that's not quite as stiff. *G. colvillei*, a hybrid of *G. tristis* (below), has 2 to 3-inch red flowers blotched with yellow on the lower petals; stems grow to 1½ feet. This species is the progenitor of a small-flowered hybrid race called "baby gladiolus," with white, pink, red, or lilac flowers typically blotched in a contrasting color.

G. primulinus grows twice as tall as *G. colvillei;* its primrose yellow blossoms are hooded instead of purely funnel shaped. It's one of the forerunners of a strain called "butterfly gladiolus": 2-foot-tall plants with wiry stems, each bearing up to 20 ruffled, somewhat hooded flowers. The 3 to 4-inch-wide blossoms are typically bicolored (the characteristic that gave this group the "butterfly" name), in a wide range of colors.

Fragrant *G. tristis* bears dainty 2 to 3-inch flowers on 1½-foot stems; color is light yellow veined with purple. (The form *G. t. concolor* is unveined.) Another fragrant species, *G. callianthus*, was until recently classed as *Acidanthera bicolor;* some growers may still offer it under that name. Blossoms are creamy white blotched with chocolate brown at the base; they have elongated, pointed petals and a more starlike shape than the blooms of other species. Variety 'Murielae' is taller, with crimson-blotched blooms.

Uses. Many gardeners grow gladiolus for cut flowers, planting them in space-efficient rows. But gladiolus set out in clumps are much more pleasing to the eye. In this arrangement, their stiffness becomes an asset; they provide striking vertical accents in mixed plantings of annuals and perennials.

Garden culture. Plant the species gladiolus and small-flowered species hybrids and strains in autumn; for the large garden hybrids, midwinter (mildest regions) to spring or even early summer is the time to plant. The large hybrids bloom approximately 100 days after planting, so if you plant corms at 1 to 2-week intervals over a period of 4 to 6 weeks, you can enjoy an extended flowering season.

Many growers prefer to plant corms as early as possible, so that flowers will finish before the annual summer onset of thrips. However, systemic insecticides can control these blossom-disfiguring pests, thus allowing attractive flowers throughout the summer. But if you'd still like your gladiolus to bloom before the onset of hottest weather, plant at these times:

• Mild West Coast: January through March
• Pacific Northwest: April through June
• Southwest low desert: November through January
• Southeast: April through June
• Midwest and Northeast: May and June

For the best looking plants and flowers, purchase corms that are high crowned for their width; broad, flat corms are older and less vigorous. Choose a bright, sunny planting area, preferably with sandy loam soil; then dig a generous amount of organic matter into the soil before you set out corms.

Planting depth varies according to corm size and soil type. Set corms deeper in light soils than in heavy ones; set thicker corms deeper than thinner ones. As a general rule, plant each corm about four times as deep as it's thick, making some adjustment for soil type. For example, you might set a 1-inch-thick corm 6 inches deep in a light soil, only 4 inches deep in a heavy soil. Spacing depends on corm diameter; position broader corms about 6 inches apart, smaller ones about 4 inches apart.

Water regularly from the time leaves emerge until the blooming season ends. If you cut flowering stems for display indoors, leave at least four leaves on each plant; these will build up the corm for the next year's performance. Stems left to bloom out in the garden should be trimmed off beneath the lowest flower after blossoms fade. Uncut stems will set seeds, diverting energy from food storage in the corm.

Some time after flowering, leaves will begin to turn yellow. At this point, withhold water and let foliage yellow completely; then dig plants, shake off soil, and cut off stems and leaves just above each corm. Destroy cut-off tops to get rid of any thrips. (In rainy-summer areas, some growers dig plants *before* foliage yellows to prevent botrytis infection, which could ruin corms in storage.)

Place corms on a flat surface in a dark, dry area and let them dry for 2 to 3 weeks. Then examine corms carefully; discard those showing lesions, irregular blotches, or discoloration, all of which could indicate disease. Remove the old, spent base from each healthy corm. If you'd like to increase a particular variety, save the small cormels for replanting; they should reach blooming size in 2 to 3 years.

Dust all corms and cormels with a powdered insecticide and keep them in a cool (40° to 50°F/4° to 10°C), dry place until planting time. To store corms, place them in onion sacks or in discarded nylon stockings or pantyhose, then hang them up; or arrange them in a single layer on shallow trays. Stack the trays if necessary, placing spacers between them to allow for air circulation.

GLORIOSA rothschildiana

GLORY LILY
CLIMBING LILY

Photo on page 46

Type of bulb: Tuber

Season of bloom: Summer

Colors: Red with yellow

Grows to: 6 feet (climbing)

When to plant: Late winter

Where to plant: Sun; filtered sun or light shade where summers are hot

How deep to plant: 4 inches

Hardiness: Tender; store indoors over winter (see below)

A number of true lilies (*Lilium*) may reach 6 feet or more; this lily relative reaches that height in a distinctive manner. The tip of each lance-shaped 5 to 7-inch leaf tapers to a tendril, which wraps around any handy support to stabilize the plant as it climbs upward. Flashy 4-inch-wide blossoms appear at the top portion of the plant, each with six recurved, wavy-edged segments in brightest red banded with yellow.

In completely frost-free regions, glory lily can survive outdoors all year. But even in these climates, it's best grown in containers. If you want the appearance of a permanent planting, just sink containers into a garden flower bed, raised bed, or planter.

Uses. Glory lily is a certain conversation piece for patio, terrace, or deck.

Container culture. Plant tubers in a horizontal position, one to a container; set them 4 inches deep in the soil mix described in directions "A" on page 91. For the longest bloom season, start tubers indoors in late winter. After danger of frost is past, move containers to an outdoor spot in full sun (filtered sunlight or lightest shade in hot-summer regions). Be sure to provide supports for the climbing stems: trellises, wire, strings, or even loose-growing shrubs or other vines.

During the growth and bloom period, water regularly and apply a liquid fertilizer every 3 weeks. Withhold water and fertilizer in autumn, when foliage begins to yellow and die back. After leaves are dry, sever dead stems and move containers to a cool (55° to 60°F/13° to 16°C), dry location for the winter. In late winter, knock tubers out of containers and repot. Or dig tubers in autumn and store them as for *Dahlia* until planting time.

HABRANTHUS

RAIN LILY

Type of bulb: True bulb

Season of bloom: Primarily summer

Colors: Pink, yellow, white

Grows to: 6 to 9 inches

When to plant: Spring

Where to plant: Sun or part shade

How deep to plant: 1 inch

Hardiness: To about 20°F/−7°C; in colder regions, grow as a container plant

(Continued on page 47)

Gladiolus *hybrid*

Haemanthus katharinae

Hemerocallis *hybrid*

Gloriosa rothschildiana

In their native habitats, these plants sprout and flower almost immediately after the ground has been moistened by summer rainfall—hence the common name "rain lily." The grassy foliage and trumpet-shaped to funnel-shaped blossoms are very similar to those of *Zephyranthes,* a close relative; but while *Zephyranthes* has upward-facing flowers, those of *Habranthus* are angled outward. Each stem bears just one blossom.

H. andersonii has 1½-inch-long yellow blooms veined with red on the outsides of the petals; both foliage and stems grow to about 6 inches. *H. texanus* looks much the same—some botanists consider it just a variety of *H. andersonii*—but its petals are more rounded and its stems reach 8 inches tall. Taller still (to 9 inches) is *H. tubispathus* (*H. robustus*), with light pink, green-throated 3-inch flowers veined in deeper pink. Like *Amaryllis,* another *Habranthus* relative, this species finishes blooming before its leaves emerge. Pink-flushed, white flowers and coarser foliage distinguish *H. juncifolius* from the other species.

Uses. Tuck clumps of *Habranthus* in the foreground of mixed groupings of summer annuals and perennials, or plant in rock gardens. In regions beyond its hardiness limit, grow *Habranthus* as a container plant.

Garden culture. Plant bulbs in well-drained soil, setting them 1 inch deep and at least 3 inches apart. Water regularly throughout the growth and bloom season. If you live in a frost-free climate, withhold water for about a month after flowers have finished; then begin regular watering again to initiate another bloom cycle. In colder areas, just let soil go dry after flowering; resume regular watering when growth begins in spring.

Plantings may be left undisturbed for many years; dig and divide only when vigor and flower quality decline or when you want to increase plantings. Replant divided bulbs immediately.

Container culture. Follow directions "C" on page 91.

HAEMANTHUS
katharinae

BLOOD LILY

Photo on page 46

Type of bulb: True bulb

Season of bloom: Late spring, summer

Colors: Coral red, pink

Grows to: 1 to 2 feet

When to plant: Late winter or early spring

Where to plant: Light shade

How deep to plant: Even with soil surface

Hardiness: Tender; store indoors over winter (see below)

Haemanthus derives the name "blood lily" from the red stains on its large white bulbs. The narrow-petaled blossoms are borne in ball-shaped clusters (up to 9 inches across) atop thick flower stems; myriad threadlike red stamens protrude from each bloom, giving flower clusters the appearance of spherical bottlebrushes. Glossy, bright green, wavy-edged leaves are 12 to 15 inches long and up to 6 inches wide.

In frost-free regions, you can plant *Haemanthus* in the ground. But even in such favored climates, this plant is usually grown in containers; for the appearance of permanent plantings, just sink containers to their rims in soil.

Uses. Good-looking foliage and splashy floral display make *Haemanthus* a prime accent plant for patio, terrace, or deck.

Garden culture. If you're growing *Haemanthus* in the ground, choose a lightly shaded spot with well-drained soil. Enrich soil with organic matter; then plant bulbs about 2 feet apart, keeping tips even with the soil surface.

During the growing season, water plants regularly and apply a liquid fertilizer monthly. Put out bait for slugs and snails. Leave clumps undisturbed indefinitely.

Container culture. For each bulb, select a container large enough to leave 2 inches between all sides of the bulb and the container edges. Fill containers with soil mix (see "C," page 91); plant bulbs so tips are even with the soil surface. Place planted containers in a fairly warm spot (no lower than 55°F/13°C at night, around 70°F/21°C during the day) receiving plenty of bright light but no direct sun. Water sparingly until leaves appear (in about 8 weeks); then water regularly throughout the growth and blooming season. Give plants monthly applications of a liquid fertilizer.

After bloom is finished, stop fertilizing and gradually cut back on water, until by midautumn plants receive no water at all. Store planted bulbs over winter in a cool (50° to 55°F/10° to 13°C), dry spot. Near the end of winter (or in early spring), tip plants out of containers and scrape some of the old soil off the root ball. Then repot in the same containers, filling in around bulbs with fresh soil. Switch to larger pots only after several years, when bulbs fill containers almost completely.

HEMEROCALLIS

DAYLILY

Photo on page 46

Type of bulb: Tuberous root

Season of bloom: Late spring, summer, autumn

Colors: Orange, yellow, lavender, purple, red, maroon, bronze, pink, cream, near-white, multicolors

Grows to: 1 to 6 feet

When to plant: Autumn or early spring

Where to plant: Sun; filtered sun or part shade where summers are hot

How deep to plant: ½ to 1 inch

Hardiness: Varies (see below)

In recent years, the old orange and yellow daylilies—indestructible components of "grandmother's garden"—have undergone a dramatic transformation at the hands of hybridizers. Standard, miniature, and small-flowered types have all been improved, the most obvious change being a greatly expanded color range. The orange and yellow shades now include soft apricot and pale yellow as well as the familiar bright hues, and you'll also find varieties with blooms in purple, lavender, red, maroon, bronze, all shades of pink, and deep to pale shades of cream (some almost white). Increased petal width and thickness are two other notable improvements. The only part that hasn't undergone change is the foliage, which gave *Hemerocallis* its old-fashioned name "corn lily": before bloom, daylilies still look like young corn plants.

Stems of standard-size daylilies generally grow 2½ to 4 feet tall, though some exceptional varieties reach heights of up to 6 feet. Miniature and small-flowered types grow just 1 to 2 feet tall. Since stems are branched along their upper portion, each one produces an abundance of flowers (fragrant, in some types).

Individual blossoms may be lily shaped or chalice shaped, from 3 to 8 inches across (about 1½ to 3 inches in the smaller varieties). Nurseries offer both single and double-flowered forms, as well as some called "spiders"; these have blooms with narrow, twisted petals. As the common name "daylily" indicates, flowers last just one day. However, some extended-bloom varieties feature blossoms that remain open into the evening and may even last until the following morning.

Bloom time usually begins in midspring, but early and late-blooming varieties are also available. By planting all three types, you can extend the spring flowering period for a month or more. Scattered bloom may occur during summer, and reblooming types put on a second display in late summer to mid-autumn.

Uses. By selecting varieties of different sizes, you can use daylilies as accents in foreground, middle, or background of any border planting. They're good for drift plantings, as well (space about 2 feet apart). Daylilies also function as a tall ground cover, even in part or light shade (they can usually endure competition from tree roots).

Garden culture. Though daylilies have a reputation for toughness and adaptability, they more than repay the gardener who gives them extra attention. Where summers are dry and hot, plant in filtered sun or part shade; in cooler regions, plant in full sun. For best results, use well-drained soil, amended with organic matter. Set roots ½ to 1 inch deep, 2 to 2½ feet apart; water regularly from spring through autumn. Divide when clumps become crowded, usually after 3 to 6 years—in autumn or early spring in hot-summer regions, in summer where summer weather is cool or where the growing season is short.

Daylilies may be evergreen, semi-evergreen, or deciduous. The deciduous types may not be totally successful in frost-free regions, but they're likely to be the hardiest (to about −35°F/−38°C) without winter protection. Evergreen kinds usually need winter protection (see page 89) where temperatures drop below −20°F/−29°C.

Container culture. The smaller daylilies are suited to container life on sunny patios, terraces, and decks. Follow directions "C" on page 91.

HIPPEASTRUM

AMARYLLIS

Photo on page 51

Type of bulb: True bulb

Season of bloom: Spring

Colors: Red, orange, pink, white, multicolors

Grows to: 2 feet

When to plant: Late autumn through midwinter

Where to plant: Sun or part shade

How deep to plant: Top of bulb neck even with soil surface

Hardiness: To about 20°F/−7°C

NOTE: Though commonly called "amaryllis," *Hippeastrum* should not be confused with the genus *Amaryllis*.

Modern "Dutch hybrid" amaryllis are the products of hybridizers in Europe and the United States, who developed them from various species native to Central and South America. Each plant produces one or two thick stems, each bearing a cluster of three to six trumpet-shaped blossoms up to 9 inches across. The broad, strap-shaped leaves may be nearly as long as the stems, but they're arching rather than upright. Flower colors range from pure white to blush and light pink to assertive, dramatic shades of crimson and orange-scarlet; the lighter colored blooms often have green throats. Many varieties are boldly veined—white veins on background colors of dark pink to red, reddish veins on white backgrounds.

Amaryllis is usually grown in containers, but can be planted in the ground where winter temperatures remain above 20°F/−7°C.

Uses. Pots of blooming amaryllis provide a focal point indoors or out; where plants are hardy in the ground, you can set them out in large clumps or dramatic drifts.

Garden culture. Set out bulbs 1 foot apart in well-drained soil enriched with organic matter; keep tops of bulb necks even with the soil surface. Water thoroughly, then keep soil just barely moist until leaves emerge. Increase watering after plants have sprouted, making sure that soil is moist at all times. Protect from slugs and snails.

After flowers have faded, cut off stalks. Withhold water when foliage yellows, letting leaves die down completely; then keep soil dry until new growth begins in autumn. Divide infrequently—only when vigor and bloom quality decline, or when you want to move or increase plantings. The best time to divide is early autumn, just before growth begins.

Container culture. Pot bulbs from midautumn through winter; the earlier you plant, the sooner flowers will appear (see also information on forcing, page 93). Select a container large enough to leave 2 inches between all sides of the bulb and the container edges. Fill container with soil mix (see directions "C" on page 91); then plant the bulb so its neck and top half are above the soil surface. Firm soil thoroughly and water well.

Move planted containers to a

room receiving plenty of light (even morning sun), with temperatures around 60° to 65°F/16° to 18°C at night, 70° to 75°F/21° to 24°C during the day. Keep soil just slightly moist until growth begins; then water regularly during the growth and bloom period. Apply liquid fertilizer monthly until foliage starts to yellow.

After flowers fade, cut off stalks to prevent seed formation. When leaves have turned completely yellow, withhold water to give bulbs the dry dormant period they need.

At planting time, remove bulbs from containers and scrape off part of the old soil; then replant in the same containers, using fresh soil. (If bulbs have outgrown their original pots, replant in larger containers.)

HYACINTHUS

HYACINTH

Photo on page 51

Type of bulb: True bulb
Season of bloom: Spring
Colors: Blue, purple, red, pink, salmon, buff, yellow, cream, white
Grows to: 6 to 12 inches
When to plant: Autumn
Where to plant: Sun
How deep to plant: 3 to 5 inches, depending on type
Hardiness: Varies (see below)

To most gardeners, "hyacinth" means just one plant: the highly fragrant, fat-spiked Dutch hybrids of *H. orientalis.* These grow to 1 foot tall; their straplike leaves may be either erect or arching. Blossom spikes look like flowering drumsticks— they're tightly crowded with small, outward-facing blooms shaped like flaring bells. Colors include pure white, clear pastels, and darker hues.

The largest bulbs (called exhibition size) produce the largest spikes; they're also the best choice for container-grown and forced flowers. The next largest size is satisfactory for outdoor planting. The smallest bulbs produce smaller, looser flower clusters—the same re-

sults you'll get from larger bulbs left in the ground from year to year.

Bulbs require subfreezing winter temperatures; with protection, they're hardy to about −30°F/ −35°C. In mild-winter regions, they quickly deteriorate after the first season; gardeners in these climates usually purchase new bulbs each year.

The Roman or French Roman hyacinth, *H. orientalis albulus,* is smaller than the *H. orientalis* hybrids and blooms earlier in the season. Each bulb may produce several slender, foot-tall stems with loose spikes of white, pale blue, or pink flowers. This hyacinth is hardy to −10°F/−23°C, and will thrive where winters offer little or no chilling.

Uses. *H. orientalis albulus* is good for naturalizing or for informal drifts beneath deciduous trees and shrubs. The Dutch hybrids provide an impressive display when massed in beds or borders, but because of their rather stiff appearance, they look rigidly formal when planted in rows.

All hyacinths can be grown in containers; the Dutch hybrids are the showiest.

Garden culture. The Dutch hybrids and *H. orientalis albulus* must be planted early enough to establish vigorous roots before the ground freezes. Where winter temperatures drop below 20°F/−7°C, set bulbs out in earliest autumn; in warmer regions, delay planting until mid to late autumn, when summerlike warmth is sure to be gone. Keep bulbs cool in the meantime; if you're planting only a few, you can store them in the vegetable crisper of your refrigerator.

Choose a sunny planting area with well-drained soil (preferably on the sandy side), and dig plenty of organic matter into the soil prior to planting. Set the largest Dutch hybrid bulbs 4 to 5 inches deep, about 5 inches apart; the smaller hybrid bulbs and those of *H. orientalis albulus* should go about 3 inches deep, 4 to 5 inches apart.

Keep soil moist after planting so roots will become established; continue to water regularly from the time leaves emerge until flowers

fade. If you plan to keep bulbs for another year (or longer), apply a granular fertilizer just as blossoms fade; remove the spent flower spikes, and maintain regular watering until foliage yellows. After foliage has died down, keep soil fairly dry during summer and until cool weather returns.

Container culture. Follow directions "B" on page 91. For information on growing bulbs indoors in "hyacinth jars," see page 93.

HYMENOCALLIS

PERUVIAN DAFFODIL

Photo on page 51

Type of bulb: True bulb
Season of bloom: Summer
Colors: White, yellow
Grows to: 2 feet
When to plant: Autumn or early winter; spring where winter temperatures drop below 10°F/−12°C
Where to plant: Sun; filtered sun or part shade where summers are hot
How deep to plant: Just beneath soil surface
Hardiness: To about 10°F/−12°C; in colder regions, dig and store over winter as for *Dahlia*

Imagine a fanciful hybrid between *Amaryllis belladonna* and a daffodil, and you'll come close to visualizing *Hymenocallis.* Like *Amaryllis,* it has strap-shaped leaves (usually about 2 feet long) and thick flower stems, each topped with several fragrant blossoms. Like daffodils, these flowers have two sets of segments: the inner ones form a separate-petaled funnel, while the outer ones are longer, spidery, and recurved.

The most common species is *H. narcissiflora* (formerly known as *H. calathina* and *Ismene calathina*), the Peruvian daffodil. Its white flowers, striped green in the throat, are carried in clusters of two to five per stem. *H. n.* 'Advance' is pure white; the hybrid 'Sulfur Queen' has blossoms of light primrose yellow with green striping in the throat. A second species, *H. caroliniana*, is native to the southeastern U.S. It has shorter leaves and smaller flowers than *H. narcissiflora*, but bears nine blooms per stem.

Uses. *Hymenocallis* is attractive in border plantings of summer-flowering annuals and perennials. It's also a good choice for containers.

Garden culture. Plant *Hymenocallis* in autumn or early winter where bulbs are hardy in the ground; in colder regions, plant in spring after all danger of frost is past.

Select a sunny location (filtered sun or part shade where summers are hot) with well-drained soil; dig a generous amount of organic matter into the soil before planting. Set in bulbs just beneath the soil surface, spacing them about 1 foot apart. Water regularly throughout the growth and flowering period; gradually withhold water when foliage starts to yellow and die down. Let bulbs remain nearly or completely dry until cool autumn conditions initiate another growth cycle.

Where winter temperatures fall below 10°F/−12°C, dig bulbs when foliage yellows, dry upside down, and store as for *Dahlia*.

Container culture. Follow directions "C" on page 91.

IPHEION uniflorum

SPRING STAR FLOWER
Photo on page 51

Type of bulb: True bulb
Season of bloom: Spring
Colors: White tinged with blue, blue
Grows to: 6 to 8 inches
When to plant: Autumn
Where to plant: Sun, part shade, or light shade
How deep to plant: 2 inches
Hardiness: To about 0°F/−18°C

This rugged little plant has an understated, wildflowerlike charm. Each bulb produces several slender stems, each bearing a 1½-inch blos-

som with six overlapping petals arranged in star fashion. The usual color is white tinged with blue, but you may be able to find the dark blue variety 'Wisley Blue' in bulb specialists' catalogs. Narrow, nearly flat bluish green leaves emit an oniony odor when bruised.

Uses. Plant spring star flower in borders or under deciduous shrubbery. Or naturalize it in woodland or among low grasses.

Garden culture. Though spring star flower prefers well-drained soil, it's not particular about the type—anything from light, sandy soil to clay is satisfactory. It's similarly unfussy about planting location: sun, part shade, and light shade are all suitable.

Plant bulbs in early to mid-autumn, 2 inches deep and 2 inches apart. Water regularly during the spring growth and blooming period, then allow soil to dry out almost completely during summer dormancy. Dig and divide infrequently, since plantings become more attractive over the years as bulbs multiply.

Container culture. Follow directions "B" on page 91.

IRIS
Photos on pages 1, 51, and 54

Type of bulb: Rhizome; true bulb
Season of bloom: Spring, summer, autumn, winter
Colors: Every color but true red; many multicolors
Grows to: 2 inches to 6 feet
When to plant: Midsummer to mid-autumn; spring
Where to plant: Sun, filtered sun, light shade, or part shade, depending on type and climate
How deep to plant: Varies depending on type
Hardiness: Varies (see below)

Mention the name *Iris*, and most people will think of the tall, showy bearded irises that are mainstays of the midspring flower display. But though these may be the most widely

planted, they constitute only one part of a highly diverse group of plants.

Despite their considerable differences, all irises have the same basic flower structure. All blossoms have three true petals (called *standards*) and three petal-like sepals (called *falls*). Standards may be upright, arching, or flaring, while falls range from flaring to drooping. Flower types fit into two broad groups: *bearded*, with a caterpillar-like tuft of hairs on each fall; and *beardless*, without such hairs. In growth habit, irises are either *rhizomatous* or *bulbous*.

Rhizomatous irises

Irises that grow from rhizomes may be bearded or beardless. Leaves are swordlike, overlapping each other to form a flat fan of foliage.

Bearded irises

Bearded irises are available in a dazzling array of colors and color combinations. Irises of this type are divided into the four main classes outlined below: *tall, median, dwarf,* and *arils and arilbreds*. Except for the arils and arilbreds, which have special needs, all bearded irises require the same basic care (see "Bearded iris culture" on page 52).

Tall bearded irises. Tall bearded irises bloom in midspring, bearing large, broad-petaled blossoms on branching stems that grow 2½ to 4 feet tall. Types designated as *reblooming* or *remontant* will bloom again in summer, autumn, or winter (depending on the variety) if grown in a favorable climate and given cultural encouragement.

Median & dwarf irises. Blossoms resemble those of tall beardeds, but on a smaller scale; stems and foliage are smaller, as well. Median is a collective term for the first four types listed below.

Border bearded irises. These are segregates from tall bearded breeding with 15 to 28-inch stems and proportionately sized flowers and foliage.

(Continued on page 52)

Hyacinthus orientalis *hybrids*

Hippeastrum *hybrids*

Ipheion uniflorum

Iris, *Japanese hybrid*

Hymenocallis narcissiflora

Miniature tall bearded irises. Height range is the same as for border beardeds (15 to 28 inches), but miniature tall beardeds have pencil-slim stems, rather narrow and short foliage, and relatively tiny flowers— only 2 to 3 inches wide. Bloom time is the same as for tall beardeds; color range is more limited. Members of this group usually have more stems per clump than the average tall bearded.

Intermediate bearded irises. Modern intermediates are hybrids of tall beardeds and standard dwarfs. Flowers are 3 to 5 inches wide, carried on 15 to 28-inch stems. The blooming season begins 1 to 3 weeks before the tall bearded season; some varieties bloom a second time in autumn. This group also includes the old, familiar "common purple" and "graveyard white" irises that flower in early spring.

Standard dwarf bearded irises. Most modern members of this group were developed from crosses of tall bearded varieties with a miniature dwarf species from central Europe. Standard dwarfs bloom even earlier than intermediates, producing a great profusion of 2 to 3-inch-wide flowers on stems 10 to 15 inches tall. There's a wide range of available colors and patterns.

Miniature dwarf bearded irises. These are the shortest of irises, reaching just 2 to 10 inches. They bear a wealth of flowers in a great variety of colors; blooms are often a bit large in proportion to the rest of the plant. Established, well-grown plants can form cushions of bloom —attractive in rock gardens, borders, and foreground plantings.

Aril & arilbred irises. The word "exotic" might have been coined especially for the aril species, which take their name from the collarlike white cap (the *aril*) on their seeds. These irises comprise two groups, Regelia and Oncocyclus; both are native to arid regions of the Near East and central Asia.

Oncocyclus species typically feature 4 to 7-inch-wide domed or globe-shaped blooms with a base color of gray, silver, lavender, gold, or maroon. In many types, the petals are intricately veined and dotted with darker hues. Flower stems are fairly short, usually reaching only about 1 foot; leaves are narrow and lightly ribbed.

Regelias have smaller and more vertical blossoms than the Oncocyclus types; both base colors and contrasting veining are in brighter shades (though *I. hoogiana* is pure blue), often with a lustrous sheen. Flower stems reach 1½ to 2½ feet, depending on care. The narrow, ribbed leaves are usually linear. Hybrids between these two groups are called Oncogelias.

All the aril species have strict cultural needs: perfect drainage (no standing water), alkaline soil, and a hot, dry summer dormant period. Oncocyclus species are the fussiest; Regelias and Oncogelias are more adaptable. All three are hardy in the ground to about −20°F/−29°C.

Arilbred irises are hybrids of aril types and tall or median bearded irises; a number of named varieties are sold, with varying percentages of aril "blood." In general, those with more aril in their ancestry have a more exotic look. Many arilbreds are nearly as easy to grow as tall beardeds, or require only the addition of lime to the soil and a little extra attention to drainage.

Bearded iris culture

Bearded irises demand good drainage; as long as rhizomes don't sit in saturated soil, they'll do well in anything from light sand to clay. (If you're growing irises in heavy soil, plant them in a raised bed or raised planting area to promote drainage.)

In cool-summer climates, plants must have full sun from spring through autumn. But where summers are hot, they may appreciate afternoon filtered sunlight or high shade. Too much shade, though, cuts way back on bloom production and interferes with the necessary summer ripening of rhizomes.

Plant rhizomes between July 1 and October 31—in July or August in cold-winter climates, in September or October where summer temperatures are high. Space rhizomes 1 to 2 feet apart; set them with tops just beneath the soil surface, spreading roots well. Growth proceeds from the end of the rhizome with leaves, so point the leafy end in the direction in which you want growth to occur initially. If the weather turns hot, shade newly planted rhizomes to prevent sunscald and subsequent rot.

After planting rhizomes, water the planting area to settle the soil and start root growth; thereafter, water judiciously until you see by new growth that plants have taken hold. Water regularly unless rain or freezing weather intercedes. From the time growth starts in late winter or early spring, water regularly until about 6 weeks after flowers fade (increases and buds for the following year are formed during the post-bloom period). During summer, plants can get by with less frequent watering—every other week in warm climates, once a month where summers are cool.

Apply a granular fertilizer as plants begin growth in late winter or early spring, then again right after the blooming season ends.

Where winter temperatures are likely to drop below −20°F/−29°C, many gardeners give plantings winter protection (see page 89) just after the ground freezes.

Clumps become overcrowded after 3 or 4 years, producing fewer flower stalks and blooms of poorer quality. When this occurs, dig clumps at the best planting time for your climate and separate old, woody rhizomes from healthy ones with good fans of leaves. Then trim leaves and roots to 6 to 8 inches and replant. If replanting in the same plot, dig plenty of organic matter into the soil before you plant.

Beardless irises

Only two main characteristics are common to all irises in this category: the lack of a beard on the falls and roots that are generally fibrous rather than fleshy. The most widely sold beardless irises are the four hybrid groups described below.

Japanese irises. Hardy to about −20°F/−29°C. Derived from *I. ensata* (formerly *I. kaempferi*), these irises are graceful, moisture-loving plants which, when grown under ideal conditions, bear the largest flowers of all irises. The narrow, upright leaves, each with a distinct midrib, are reminiscent of rushes. Above the foliage clumps, 4 to 12-inch flowers float on stems up to 4 feet tall. Blossoms are fairly flat, either single (standards small and distinct in appearance from falls) or double (standards and falls of about equal size, shape, and markings). Colors include white and all shades of purple, violet, blue, and pink; light-colored blooms are often intricately marked, veined, or striped. Flowering begins in late spring.

Japanese irises must have rich soil and copious nonalkaline moisture from the time growth begins until the blooming season ends. Grow them at pond edges or in boxes, pots, or buckets of soil sunk halfway to the rim in the water of pond or pool. If you water them very faithfully, they'll also succeed in heavy garden soil. Where summers are cool, plant in full sun; in warm-summer regions, choose a spot receiving high or dappled afternoon shade.

Set out rhizomes in autumn or spring, 2 inches deep and 1½ feet apart, pointing the leafy ends in the direction you want growth to take. (Or plant up to three rhizomes per 12-inch container.) Divide crowded clumps in late summer or early autumn; replant as quickly as possible.

Louisiana irises. Hardy to about 0°F/−18°C. The progenitors of this group are three or more species native to swamps and moist lowlands, primarily along the Gulf Coast. Leaves are long, linear, and unribbed; graceful, flattish blossoms are carried on 2 to 5-foot stems. The range of flower colors and patterns is nearly as extensive as that of the tall beardeds.

Though the species come from milder climates, some varieties have been successful as far north as South Dakota. Plants will thrive in rich, well-watered garden soil as well as at pond margins; both soil and water should be neutral to acid. Full sun is best in cool and mild-summer areas, but where summer heat is intense, chose a spot receiving light afternoon shade. Plant in late summer, setting rhizomes 1 inch deep and 1½ to 2 feet apart.

Where ground freezes in winter, give plants winter protection (page 89).

Siberian irises. Hardy to about −30°F/−35°C. The most widely sold members of this group are named hybrids derived from *I. sibirica* and *I. sanguinea*. All have narrow, almost grasslike deciduous foliage and slender flower stems. Depending on the variety, leaf length ranges from 1 to 3 feet, stem height from about 14 inches to nearly 4 feet. In midspring, each stem bears two to five blossoms with upright standards and flaring to drooping falls. Colors include white and every shade of violet, purple, lavender, wine, pink, and blue; several recent hybrids are light yellow.

Plant Siberian irises in early spring or late summer in cold-winter regions, in autumn where summers are hot and winters mild to moderate. Plant in sun (light shade where summers are hot) in good, neutral to acid soil; set in rhizomes 1 to 2 inches deep, 1 to 2 feet apart. Water generously from the time growth begins until the bloom period is over. Divide infrequently; plants look most attractive in well-established clumps. Dig and divide (in late summer or early autumn) only when old clumps begin to show hollow centers.

Spuria irises. Hardy to about −30°F/−35°C. In general flower form, Spurias are almost identical to florists' Dutch irises. The older members of this group have yellow or white-and-yellow flowers, but modern hybrids show a greatly expanded range of colors: blue, lavender, gray, orchid, tan, bronze, brown, purple, earthy red, and near black, often with a prominent yellow spot on the falls. Blossoms are held closely against 3 to 6-foot flower stems. The narrow, dark green leaves grow upright to 3 to 4 feet.

Plant these irises in late summer or early autumn, in a full-sun location with good soil. Set rhizomes 1 inch deep, 1½ to 2 feet apart; water regularly from the time growth begins until flowering is over. Most Spurias need very little water during summer. Give plants winter protection (see page 89) where temperature drops below −20°F/−29°C.

Divide plantings infrequently—only when they become overcrowded. Dig and replant rhizomes in late summer or early autumn.

Bulbous irises

Like bearded irises, all bulbous irises have foliage that grows in flattened fans, but leaves tend to be more grasslike and rounder in cross section. In summer, the leaves die back and bulbs enter dormancy. At this time, they can be dug and stored until planting time in autumn.

Dutch irises

Dutch bulb growers developed these hybrids from several Mediterranean species. All are hardy to about −10°F/−23°C and bear sturdy, rather stiff blossoms with erect standards and down-curving falls. Flowers are 3 to 4 inches across, carried on stiff 1½ to 2-foot stems; they're available in white and various bright, clear colors, including blue, purple, mauve, bronze, yellow, and orange. (Some types have bicolored blooms.) In warm-winter climates, flowering comes in March and April; where winters are colder, blossoms appear in May and June.

Choose a sunny planting area with well-drained soil, preferably in a part of the garden that can remain unwatered over the summer. Plant bulbs in October or November, 4 inches deep and 3 to 4 inches apart. Give plenty of water from the time leaves emerge until about a month after flowers finish; then withhold water and let foliage die.

Where summers are dry (and the planting area won't receive summer watering), you can leave bulbs in the ground for several years. Dig and divide when plants show a decline in vigor and bloom quality. But where there's summer watering or rainfall, dig bulbs after leaves are dead and hold until planting time in autumn (don't keep bulbs out of the ground for more than 2 months).

Though it's usually sold as a Dutch iris (and needs the same care), the variety 'Wedgwood' is larger, taller, and earlier blooming by about 2 weeks (at 'King Alfred'

(Continued on page 55)

Iris, *Dutch hybrid*

Iris, *Spuria hybrid*

Iris, *tall bearded hybrids*

Ixia maculata

daffodil time). It succeeds only where winter temperatures remain above 10°F/ − 12°C.

Spanish irises

This group of irises is derived from species native to Spain. Its members have the same cultural needs and general appearance as Dutch irises, though plants tend to be smaller flowered, shorter, and slimmer. Spanish irises come into bloom about 2 weeks later than the Dutch types.

English irises

All the available named varieties and color variations of English irises are derived solely from *I. xiphioides* (sometimes sold as *I. latifolia*). This species gained the name "English iris" because it was first grown as an ornamental plant in England; its true home, though, is in the moist meadows of northeastern Spain and the Pyrenees Mountains.

Flower stems may reach 1½ feet tall. In early summer, each bears two velvety-textured blooms of white, mauve, maroon, blue-purple, or blue (bulb specialists may list varieties of specific colors). Flower form is similar to that of Dutch irises, but blossoms are a bit larger, with much broader falls.

English irises do best in a climate with cool to moderate summers. Plant bulbs as soon as they're available in nurseries (usually October or November); choose a location in full sun (or in part shade, where summers are warm to hot), with cool, moist, acid soil. General cultural requirements are the same as those of Dutch irises, but English irises don't need complete dryness after flowering. Bulbs are hardy to about − 10°F/ − 23°C.

Reticulata irises

The several species and varieties belonging to the Reticulata section are characterized by a netted outer covering on the bulb. They're small, slim plants (most no taller than 8 inches), classic choices for rock gardens and pathway border plantings. Bulbs are hardy to about − 10°F/

− 23°C, but require some subfreezing winter temperatures to thrive.

Depending on the severity of the winter, flowering time varies from midwinter to early spring. Blossoms are 2 to 3 inches across. Slender, sometimes spikelike leaves may appear simultaneously with the flowers or emerge just after bloom ceases.

The group's best known member is *I. reticulata,* with flowers of pale to violet blue, red-violet, or white. Blossoms of *I. histrioides* and its variety *I. h. major* are light to medium blue, with darker blue spots on the falls. Bright yellow *I. danfordiae* differs from the others in both flower color and flower form—standards are almost nonexistent. Bulb specialists may offer other species and varieties.

Reticulata irises appreciate a full-sun location with well-drained soil. Set out bulbs in autumn, 3 to 4 inches deep and as far apart. Plants need regular watering from autumn through spring, but soil should be kept dry during the bulbs' summer dormant period. Dig and divide only when vigor and flower quality deteriorate.

IXIA

AFRICAN CORN LILY

Photo on page 54

Type of bulb: Corm

Season of bloom: Late spring

Colors: Pink, red, orange, yellow, cream, white, green

Grows to: 16 to 24 inches

When to plant: Autumn; spring where winter temperatures fall below 10°F/ − 12°C

Where to plant: Sun

How deep to plant: 2 to 4 inches

Hardiness: To about 20°F/ − 7°C; to about 10°F/ − 12°C with winter protection (see page 89); in colder regions, grow as a container plant or dig and store over winter as for *Gladiolus*

Ixia's clumps of narrow, almost grasslike leaves give rise to wiry stems topped by short spikes of bright, cheery, 2-inch flowers. Each

six-petaled blossom opens out nearly flat in full sun, but remains cup shaped or closed on overcast days.

Most of the ixias available at nurseries are hybrids involving *I. maculata;* the color range is extensive, but most types have dark-centered blossoms regardless of the basic color. A lovely curiosity is *I. viridiflora,* with purple-centered bluish green flowers.

Uses. *Ixia* offers bright-colored wildflower charm in the foreground of mixed plantings or naturalized in sunny drifts where summers are dry.

Garden culture. Plant *Ixia* in a sunny spot with light, well-drained soil. In regions where winter low temperatures usually remain above 20°F/ − 7°C, plant corms in early autumn, setting them about 2 inches deep and 3 inches apart. Where winter lows may dip down to 10°F/ − 12°C, plant after November 1; set corms 4 inches deep, then cover the planting area with winter mulch (see page 89). The later planting time, greater planting depth, and mulch keep corms from sending up leaves that would be damaged by cold.

Where temperatures fall below 10°F/ − 12°C, plant corms in spring. They'll flower in early summer— later than autumn-planted corms.

Water plants regularly during the growing and blooming period, then let soil go dry when foliage yellows. If corms are planted among drought-tolerant plants or by themselves, you can leave them undisturbed in dry-summer areas where they're hardy in the ground. After several years, or when planting becomes crowded and flower quality decreases, dig corms in summer and store as for *Gladiolus* until planting time in autumn.

Where there's summer watering or summer rainfall, and in regions where corms are not hardy in the ground, dig them after foliage dies back and store as for *Gladiolus* until the best planting time for your climate.

Container culture. Plant corms close together and about 1 inch deep in a deep container. Follow directions "B" on page 91.

LACHENALIA

CAPE COWSLIP

Photo on page 59

Type of bulb: True bulb
Season of bloom: Late winter, early spring
Colors: Yellow, orange, red, coral
Grows to: 10 to 15 inches
When to plant: Late summer or early autumn
Where to plant: Sun; part or light shade where summers are hot
How deep to plant: 1 to 1½ inches
Hardiness: To about 20°F/−7°C

Mild-winter gardeners searching for a hyacinth-like plant that persists from year to year find just what they want in *Lachenalia.* Each bulb usually produces just two broad leaves (brown-spotted in some kinds), succulent and strap shaped. Spikes of pendant, tubular blossoms appear at the tips of thick flowering stems.

The most common *Lachenalia* species is *L. aloides* (*L. tricolor*), with yellow flowers tipped in red and green; several named varieties and hybrids offer orange-yellow or red-orange blossoms. Flower stems reach 10 to 12 inches. *L. bulbiferum* (*L. pendula*) is taller (to about 15 inches), with red and yellow flowers tipped in purple.

Uses. Lachenalia is at home in rock gardens and border plantings, as well as in containers.

Garden culture. Where summers are cool or mild, plant bulbs in a sunny spot; in hot-summer climates, choose an area in part or light shade. Set out bulbs in well-drained soil, 3 inches apart and 1 to 1½ inches deep; water sparingly until growth begins, then water regularly throughout the growing and blooming season. Cut back on water when foliage starts to yellow, and keep soil as dry as possible during the summer dormant period. Resume light watering in early autumn. Protect plants from slugs and snails.

Container culture. Plant bulbs close together, with tips just beneath the soil surface, in the container soil mixture described under directions "A" on page 91. Place potted bulbs in a cool, shaded spot; indoors, place in a cool room (maximum 55°F/13°C at night, 65°F/18°C during the day) receiving sunlight for half the day. Water just enough to keep soil moist until growth begins. As growth becomes active, increase water and move outdoor containers into a warmer location in light shade or filtered sunlight. From the time flower stalks show until bloom ceases, apply a liquid fertilizer every other week. Stop watering when leaves start to yellow; keep soil dry throughout summer. In late summer, knock bulbs out of their containers and repot in fresh soil.

LAPEIROUSIA

Photo on page 59

Type of bulb: Corm
Season of bloom: Late spring
Colors: Red, white
Grows to: 6 to 12 inches
When to plant: Early autumn; early spring where winter temperatures fall below 0°F/−18°C
Where to plant: Sun or part shade
How deep to plant: 1 to 2 inches
Hardiness: To about 0°F/−18°C; in colder regions, dig and store over winter as for *Gladiolus*

The most common *Lapeirousia* species, *L. laxa* (*L. cruenta*), clearly shows its kinship to *Watsonia*. The swordlike leaves grow in flattened fans; star-shaped 1-inch flowers with tubular bases face in one direction from a short, sometimes slightly branched, spike. The usual color is red with darker markings at the throat, but a white form 'Alba' is sometimes available.

Uses. Plant *Lapeirousia* in clumps or drifts, in the foreground of mixed annual and perennial plantings; or naturalize it in light shade.

Garden culture. Plant corms 1 to 2 inches deep, 3 inches apart, in well-drained soil—in early autumn where corms are hardy in the ground, in early spring in colder regions. Water regularly through the growing season, but taper off during the summer dormant period.

Where corms can winter in the ground, dig and separate infrequently: appearance improves as plantings multiply. (Self-sown seedling plants may help increase the planting.) In colder climates, dig in early autumn and store over winter as for *Gladiolus*.

Container culture. Follow directions "B" on page 91.

LEUCOCORYNE ixioides

GLORY-OF-THE-SUN

Type of bulb: True bulb
Season of bloom: Early spring
Color: Blue
Grows to: 1 to 1½ feet
When to plant: Autumn
Where to plant: Sun
How deep to plant: 3 inches
Hardiness: To about 20°F/−7°C

This South American native may not always be easy to locate in nurseries, but for mild-winter gardeners it's worth the effort. Glory-of-the-sun merits planting for fragrance alone—and its looks are equally entrancing. Waxy blue flowers are borne in loose clusters atop wiry stems; each star-shaped blossom is 1 to 2 inches across, with a white center and prominent gold anthers. The foot-long foliage is grasslike.

Uses. Glory-of-the-sun is a good choice for naturalizing or planting in rock gardens or borders of drought-tolerant plants.

Garden culture. Plant glory-of-the-sun in full sun, setting bulbs 3 inches deep and 3 inches apart. Fast-draining soil is essential; bulbs will not endure saturated soil during their autumn-through-spring growth period. Give plants little or no summer water—after foliage dies down, bulbs need a warm, dry dormant period. Resume regular watering in early autumn. This plant increases only by seed, so you never need to dig and divide.

A peculiar trait of glory-of-the-sun is that bulbs tend to move downward, a bit each year, until they become too deep to grow. You can halt their migration by laying a wire screen across the bottom of the planting area, or by planting bulbs in containers, then sinking containers in the ground.

Container culture. Follow directions "C" on page 91.

LEUCOJUM

SNOWFLAKE

Photo on page 59

Type of bulb: True bulb

Season of bloom: Autumn, winter, spring

Colors: White with green; pink

Grows to: 6 to 18 inches

When to plant: Autumn; summer (from divisions)

Where to plant: Part or light shade; or sun during bloom time, part or light shade during rest of year

How deep to plant: 3 inches

Hardiness: Varies (see below)

Dainty appearance belies a tough constitution: snowflakes, where adapted, are among the most tolerant of bulbs. Most common in mild climates is *L. aestivum*; it's hardy to −30°F/−35°C, but grows in both frost-free and colder areas. Though it's commonly called "summer snowflake," the name · is misleading: in warmer parts of the West and Southwest, flowering begins in late November and continues into winter. In cold-winter regions, blossoms appear in midspring. Narrow, strap-shaped leaves grow 1 to 1½ feet long; flower stems are equally long (or longer), each carrying three to five pendant, six-segmented white bells. The pointed tip of each blossom segment is marked with green. Variety 'Gravetye Giant' is a bit taller and larger flowered than the species.

The spring snowflake, *L. vernum*, blooms in midwinter to earliest spring, depending on climate. Like *L. aestivum*, it's hardy to −30°F/−35°C, but needs definite winter cold to thrive. It's generally unsuccessful where winter temperatures are warmer than 20°F/−7°C. Blooms are similar to those of summer snowflake, but each foot-tall stem bears just one blossom.

Autumn-flowering *L. autumnale*, hardy to −10°F/−23°C, is less widely grown than *L. vernum* and *L. aestivum*. Its blossoms, usually borne just one to each 6-inch stem, are tinted pink. Grasslike foliage appears after flowers finish.

Uses. Naturalize snowflakes under deciduous trees or shrubs; use clumps along lightly shaded pathways.

Garden culture. Plant all species in autumn. Set out bulbs in well-drained soil, about 3 inches deep and 4 inches apart. Water regularly from planting time until foliage yellows and dies down in late spring of the next year. Less water is needed during the summer dormant period; *L. aestivum* will thrive with no summer watering.

Leave clumps undisturbed until diminished growth and flower quality indicate overcrowding. Dig and separate in summer; replant immediately.

LILIUM

LILY

Photos on pages 13 and 59

Type of bulb: True bulb

Season of bloom: Spring, summer, autumn

Colors: Yellow, orange, red, maroon, pink, cream, white, lilac, purple, pale green, multicolors

Grows to: 1 to 8 feet

When to plant: Autumn, as soon as available

Where to plant: Filtered sun, part shade, or light shade; full sun only where summers are cool or overcast

How deep to plant: Varies depending on type

Hardiness: Varies (see below)

The word "aristocratic" has been aptly used to describe lilies. From foot-tall species in the wild to 6-foot modern hybrids in the summer flower border, all lilies possess a highbred polish and elegance.

For centuries, wild lily species and species hybrids have been garden favorites in many parts of the world. But the lilies most widely grown today weren't developed until this century, when growers and hybridizers embarked on intensive breeding programs. By selectively combining species, hybridizers produced varieties and strains with new colors, new flower forms, and greater health and vigor than their species parents. And as the plants themselves were improved, so were the techniques used to grow them. The net result was a great gain for home gardeners: the new, more robust lilies were much easier to grow.

Types of lilies

Specialists' catalogs list a potentially bewildering assortment of lily hybrids (and sometimes species). However, the official classification of lilies establishes some order in this seeming chaos by separating the group into nine divisions: eight reasonably cohesive hybrid categories, and a ninth category strictly for species.

The nine divisions are listed below, along with the approximate hardiness of the plants in each group. For fuller descriptions of each division, consult a lily or bulb specialist catalog.

• Division 1. Asiatic Hybrids. Hardy to about −30°F/−35°C.

• Division 2. Martagon Hybrids. Hardy to about −30°F/−35°C.

• Division 3. Candidum Hybrids. Hardy to about −20°F/−29°C.

• Division 4. American Hybrids. Hardiness varies, according to parent species, from −10° to −30°F/ −23° to −35°C.

• Division 5. Longiflorum Hybrids. Hardiness varies; most survive to about −20F/−29°C.

• Division 6. Aurelian Hybrids. Hardy to about −30°F/−35°C.

• Division 7. Oriental Hybrids. Hardy to about −20°F/−29°C.

• Division 8. Miscellaneous hybrids. Hardiness varies.

• Division 9. Species lilies. Hardiness varies.

(Continued on next page)

Uses. Lilies are spendid components in mixed plantings of annuals, perennials, and even shrubs. And since they're available in such a great height range, you can use them in foreground, center, or background. When planted in clumps, many types have the mass of a shrub.

Many of the smaller species lilies are excellent candidates for naturalizing; try setting them out in drifts under high shade of deciduous trees, along with smaller types of ferns and other low plants that will keep their roots cool.

Garden culture. Lilies have three basic cultural needs: deep, loose, well-drained, fertile soil; ample moisture all year (lilies never completely stop growing); and coolness and shade at their roots, but sun or filtered sun for blooming tops.

Begin by choosing a planting area with the right kind of light. Where summer is cool, foggy, or overcast, you can plant in full sun, but in most other climates filtered sun or light shade is better. Morning sun is especially important—drying leaves quickly helps prevent botrytis. Be sure, though, that plants' bases will not receive bright, direct sun for any length of time. Also avoid planting in windy locations.

Before planting, prepare the soil well: dig it to a depth of about 1 foot and add plenty of organic matter. The simplest method is to dig the soil; then spread a 3 to 4-inch layer of organic matter on the surface; and then scatter on a granular fertilizer, using the amount the package directs. Thoroughly dig the organic matter and fertilizer into the loosened soil.

It's best to plant bulbs as soon as you can after you get them. If you must delay, keep bulbs in a cool place. Before planting, check bulbs carefully; if they look shriveled, place them in moist sand or peat moss until the scales plump up and roots form. Also cut off any injured portions and dust the cuts with sulfur.

All lily bulbs should be planted about 1 foot apart, but planting depth varies according to bulb size and rooting habit. Some lilies send out roots only from their bulbs, but many others produce roots from stems as well (the hybrids in Divisions 1, 2, 4, 5, 6, and 7, for example). Stem-rooting types need deeper planting than those that root from bulbs alone. A general rule for stem-rooting types is to cover smaller bulbs with 2 to 3 inches of soil, medium-size bulbs with 3 to 4 inches, and larger bulbs with 4 to 6 inches. Division 3 lilies (*L. candidum* and hybrids) root from bulbs only; plant these just 1 inch deep. If you're uncertain about correct planting depth, set bulbs shallower rather than deeper—lilies have contractile roots that will gradually pull bulbs down to the proper depth.

Gophers are fond of lily bulbs. If they're a problem in your area, see "Foiling the spoilers," page 85.

Water well after planting, then mulch the soil with 2 to 3 inches of organic matter to conserve moisture and keep soil cool. Since most lilies never really enter a dormant period, they need constant moisture all year round; try to keep soil moist to a depth of at least 6 inches. You can taper off on watering a bit after tops turn yellow in autumn, but never let roots go completely dry. (The exceptions to the constant-watering rule are Division 3 lilies—*L. candidum* and hybrids—and certain other species native to dry-summer parts of southern Europe and western Asia. Let these types go dry during mid to late summer.) Avoid overhead watering if possible, since it can topple tall types when they're in flower.

Remove faded flowers to prevent seed formation, but don't cut back stems until leaves have yellowed in autumn.

During the period of active growth and bloom, watch for and control aphids: these pests spread an incurable virus disease (symptoms include mottling on the leaves). Dig and destroy afflicted plants to prevent the spread of infection. In humid-summer regions, botrytis is another problem to watch out for.

When clumps become crowded and bloom quality declines, you can dig and divide lilies in early spring, just before growth begins, or in autumn after foliage has yellowed. (Division 3 lilies are again an exception; dig and divide these during their dormant period in summer.) If you simply need to transplant a lily clump without dividing it, you can do so at any time—even when plants are in full bloom. Just be sure to dig very carefully and replant immediately.

Container culture. Lily roots need plenty of room, so always use deep containers. Plant one bulb in a 5 to 7-inch pot, up to five in a 14 to 16-inch pot. Fill containers one-third full of either of the soil mixes described in "B" on page 91; then set in bulbs, with roots spread out and pointing downward. Cover bulbs with an additional inch of soil, water thoroughly, and place in cool, shady spot. Keep soil only moderately moist during the rooting period. When top growth appears, water more frequently; as stems elongate, gradually add more soil until containers are filled to 1 inch beneath the rim. Then move containers to a partly shaded location for the bloom period. Apply liquid fertilizer monthly during the growth and bloom season.

After flowers fade, cut back on water, but never let soil dry out (except for Division 3 lilies). Repot when bulbs crowd their containers.

LYCORIS

SPIDER LILY

Photo on page 14

Type of bulb: True bulb

Season of bloom: Late summer, autumn

Colors: Red, pink, yellow, white

Grows to: 1½ to 2 feet

When to plant: Late summer

Where to plant: Sun

How deep to plant: Top of bulb neck just beneath soil surface

Hardiness: Varies (see below); in regions beyond hardiness limits, grow as container plants

Spider lily has much in common with its more common relative *Amaryllis belladonna*. Narrow, strap-shaped leaves appear in spring and

(Continued on page 60)

Lapeirousia laxa

Lachenalia aloides

Lilium, *Asiatic Hybrids*

Leucojum aestivum

grow throughout the season, then die down completely during summer. The smooth flower stalks emerge shortly after foliage disappears, each bearing a cluster of lily-like blossoms in late summer and early autumn. Blossoms are funnel shaped or wide open, with narrow, pointed petals; most have long, projecting, spidery-looking stamens.

Golden spider lily, *L. africana* (*L. aurea*), is the tenderest species: it survives outdoors only where winter temperatures remain above 25°F/ −4°C. Its bright yellow, 3-inch flowers appear in early autumn. The best known species, *L. radiata*, is somewhat tougher, tolerating temperatures as low as 10°F/−12°C. It blooms in late summer, bearing coral red flowers with a gold sheen to the petals. (There's also a white-flowered variety, 'Alba'.)

The hardiest of common *Lycoris* species (to −10°F/−23°C) is fragrant *L. squamigera*. It was once classed as *Amaryllis hallii*, and its late summer blossoms—3 inches across, bright pink to rosy lilac—greatly resemble those of *Amaryllis belladonna*.

Uses. *Lycoris* provides accent color among other plants that tolerate dry soil in summer.

Garden culture. Choose a sunny planting area that can remain dry during the bulbs' summer dormant period. Plant bulbs in well-drained soil about 1 foot apart, with tops of bulb necks just beneath the soil surface. Water regularly while plants are growing, but withhold water and let soil go dry when foliage begins to wither.

Dig and divide just after bloom only when you want to move or increase plantings.

Container culture. In regions beyond their hardiness limits, all *Lycoris* species can be grown in containers and overwintered indoors in a brightly lit room or greenhouse where temperatures fall between 40°F/4°C and 65°F/18°C. Follow directions "C" on page 91.

While leaves are growing in winter and spring, water regularly and apply liquid fertilizer monthly.

Move containers outdoors when danger of frost is past. Gradually cut back on water from late spring into summer, during which times leaves will start to yellow. When foliage has died down, stop watering; resume when flower stalks emerge. Repot every 3 to 5 years, when bulbs crowd their containers.

MUSCARI

GRAPE HYACINTH

Photo on page 62

Type of bulb: True bulb
Season of bloom: Early spring
Colors: Blue, white; also greenish brown, lilac
Grows to: 8 to 18 inches
When to plant: Early autumn
Where to plant: Sun or light shade
How deep to plant: 2 inches
Hardiness: To about −40°F/−40°C

Though more modest in flower than its relative the true hyacinth (*Hyacinthus*), *Muscari* makes up for the difference in its profusion of blooms and ease of culture. Most species bear fragrant, urn-shaped blossoms carried in short, tight spikes atop short stems; in blue-flowered forms, the blossom clusters resemble bunches of grapes. The fleshy, grass-like leaves usually emerge in autumn, but foliage is rarely damaged by low temperatures.

M. armeniacum and its varieties are the most widely available grape hyacinths. The species has floppy foliage and bright blue flowers on 8-inch spikes; 'Early Giant' is deep blue, while 'Blue Spike' has light blue double blossoms. 'Cantab' is light blue, with shorter stems and neater foliage than the species.

The Italian grape hyacinth, *M. botryoides*, bears medium blue flowers (white, in variety 'Album') on stems to 1 foot tall. *M. tubergenianum*, called the "Oxford and Cambridge hyacinth," takes its common name from its two-toned flower spikes. Blossoms are light blue (Cambridge) at the top of the spike, dark blue (Oxford) in the lower portion. Stems reach just 8 inches.

M. comosum, the fringe or tassel hyacinth, is a complete departure from the other species. Its flowers, borne in loose clusters on 1 to 1½-foot-tall stems, have an odd shredded appearance. In the species, blossoms are greenish brown on the lower part of the spike, bluish purple in the upper portion; in variety 'Monstrosum', the petals resemble lilac-colored shredded coconut.

Uses. Naturalizing is a "natural" for grape hyacinths. They'll readily produce a carpet of bloom under deciduous trees and shrubs, along paths, or in transitional areas between garden and meadow. They're also prime container candidates.

Garden culture. Plant bulbs about 2 inches deep and 3 inches apart in well-drained soil. Water regularly during autumn, winter, and spring; in summer, when leaves have died down and bulbs are dormant, give less water or even no water at all.

Bulbs increase fairly rapidly, and many species also spread by self-sown seeds. When clumps become crowded to the extent that vigor and flower quality decline, dig and divide bulbs in early autumn.

Container culture. Follow directions "B" on page 91.

NARCISSUS

DAFFODIL
JONQUIL

Photos on pages 1, 4, 15, 16, and 62

Type of bulb: True bulb
Season of bloom: Winter, spring
Colors: Yellow, white, cream, multicolors
Grows to: 3 to 18 inches
When to plant: Autumn; summer (from divisions)
Where to plant: Sun; where summers are hot, ideal location receives sun during bloom time, part or light shade during rest of year
How deep to plant: 3 to 6 inches, depending on size of bulb
Hardiness: To about −30°F/−35°C, with some exceptions

Generations of gardeners have considered daffodils and other members of *Narcissus* the most trouble-free of spring-flowering bulbs. Given minimum care at planting time, bulbs will grow, bloom, increase—in other words, *thrive*—with virtually no further attention. They do not require summer watering (but will take it), need only infrequent division (and will even survive without it), and are totally unappetizing to the rodents that find tulips, for example, such a treat. They have just two principal enemies: encroaching shade, which can adversely affect performance; and the narcissus bulb fly (see page 94), which, if unchecked, can seriously erode the bulb population.

All plants variously called "daffodil," "narcissus," and "jonquil" are properly *Narcissus*. But in gardener's terms, *daffodil* refers only to the large-flowered kinds, while *narcissus* denotes the small-flowered (and usually early-blooming) types that bear their blossoms in clusters of four or more per stem. *Jonquil* correctly refers only to *N. jonquilla* and its hybrids.

All *Narcissus* have the same basic flower structure. Each bloom has six outer "petals" (the *perianth*) and a central petal-like structure (the *corona*) which usually forms an elongated tube or a shallower, cup-like structure. Color range is also fairly consistent across the genus: the perianth may be orange, yellow, cream, or white, while the corona is white, cream, yellow, orange, red, pink, or a light color bordered by yellow, pink, orange, or red.

Types of Narcissus. Despite their general similarities in color and form, *Narcissus* blossoms do vary in appearance from one species or hybrid type to another. Based on this variation and on botanical relationships, the Royal Horticultural Society of England has established 12 divisions of *Narcissus*. Except where noted, all are hardy to about −30°F/−35°C.

• Division 1. Trumpet daffodils. Corona as long or longer than the perianth segments; one flower to each stem. Best known trumpet daffodil is yellow 'King Alfred'.

• Divison 2. Large-cupped daffodils. Corona shorter than the perianth segments, but always more than one-third their length; one flower to each stem.

• Division 3. Small-cupped daffodils. Corona no more than one-third the length of the perianth segments; one flower to each stem.

• Division 4. Double daffodils. Corona segments greatly multiplied, and separate rather than joined together. Blossom has a fluffy appearance and looks more like a peony than a typical daffodil. One flower to each stem.

• Division 5. Triandrus Hybrids. Derivatives of *N. triandrus*. Corona at least two-thirds the length of the perianth segments; several flowers to each stem.

• Division 6. Cyclamineus Hybrids. Derivatives of *N. cyclamineus;* early-flowering forms carrying one flower on each stem. Perianth segments are strongly recurved (as though facing a stiff headwind); 'February Gold' is the best known example.

• Division 7. Jonquilla Hybrids. Derivatives of *N. jonquilla*. Each stem bears two to four small, fragrant flowers. Foliage is often rushlike.

• Division 8. Tazetta & Tazetta Hybrids. Derivatives of *N. tazetta*. Hardy to about 10°F/−12°C. This division includes all the early-blooming, cluster-flowering types popularly known as "narcissus." Each stem bears four to eight or more highly fragrant flowers with short coronas. Many types have a white perianth and a yellow corona, but there are other color combinations. *N. tazetta* 'Orientalis', the Chinese sacred lily, has a light yellow perianth and a darker yellow corona, while *N. t.* 'Paper-white' is pure white. 'Grand Soleil d'Or' has a yellow perianth and an orange corona.

• Division 9. Poeticus narcissus. Derivatives of *N. poeticus*. Perianth segments are white; very short, broad corona is in a contrasting color, usually with red edges.

• Division 10. Species, their naturally occurring forms, & wild hybrids. Included here are numerous miniature types popular with collectors and rock garden enthusiasts. Prominent among these are the following:

N. bulbocodium (hoop petticoat daffodil). Hardy to about −10°F/−23°C. Six-inch-tall stems bear small yellow flowers with flaring coronas and almost threadlike perianth segments. Foliage is grassy.

N. cyclamineus. Hardy to about −10°F/−23°C. Small flowers, one to each 6 to 12-inch stem, have strongly recurved perianth segments and tubular coronas.

N. jonquilla (jonquil). Small, fragrant blossoms are borne in clusters of two to six, on stems up to 1 foot tall. Cuplike corona is short in relation to the perianth segments; foliage is rushlike.

N. triandrus (angel's-tears). Plants have rushlike foliage and one to six small, white to pale yellow flowers per stem. Corona is at least half as long as the perianth segments. The tallest forms of this species reach 10 inches.

N. asturiensis (often sold as *N.* 'Miniature'). Pale yellow flowers, only 1 inch long, are miniature trumpet daffodils (see Division 1, above). Plant height is just 3 inches.

• Division 11. Split-corona hybrids. The corona is split for at least one-third of its length into two or more segments.

• Division 12. Miscellaneous. This category contains all *Narcissus* that don't fit the other 11 divisions.

Uses. Daffodils and other *Narcissus* are among the most versatile of bulbs. Plant them in mixed borders of annuals and perennials, under deciduous trees and shrubs, or even beneath ground covers that grow loosely enough to let plants come through. You can also naturalize bulbs in high shade beneath deciduous trees or in open, grassy meadowland.

The small species *Narcissus* can be permanent container residents; all other types are attractive container plants for just one season, after which they should be moved to the garden.

Garden culture. When buying daffodil bulbs, look for solid, heavy bulbs with no injury to the basal plate. Bulbs designated as "double nose" will give you the most and largest flowers the first season after planting.

(Continued on page 63)

Narcissus tazetta *'Paper-white'*

Narcissus jonquilla *hybrid*

Narcissus triandrus albus

Narcissus, *Division 4 hybrid*

Muscari armeniacum

In most regions, it's best to plant in late summer or early autumn, as soon as bulbs become available. But in areas with long, warm autumns and fairly mild winters, put off planting until soil has cooled in midautumn.

Select a planting area that will be in full sun while bulbs are blooming, keeping in mind that blossoms will face the source of light. One traditional and attractive location is under high-branching deciduous trees. After bloom has ended, shade or part shade can actually be beneficial to plants, especially in hot-summer regions.

For all types of *Narcissus*, good drainage is the primary soil requirement. Dig plenty of organic matter into the soil prior to planting: this will improve drainage in heavy soils and aid moisture retention in light ones.

Plant bulbs approximately twice as deep as they're tall; this measures out to 5 or 6 inches deep for large bulbs, 3 to 5 inches deep for smaller sizes. Space bulbs 6 to 8 inches apart, so they can increase for a number of years without crowding each other.

Water newly planted bulbs well to initiate root growth. In many parts of the country, autumn and winter will be wet (or snowy) enough to take care of bulbs' water requirements until flowering time or later. But if rainfall is inadequate, keep plantings well watered between rains: plants need plenty of moisture during their growing and flowering period, especially after foliage has broken through the ground.

After flowers have faded, continue to water plants regularly until foliage begins to turn yellow. Then stop watering, let foliage die down, and keep soil dry (or fairly dry) until autumn.

Slugs and snails can be bothersome to foliage, stems, and flowers, but the most serious pest for all types of *Narcissus* is the narcissus bulb fly. An adult fly resembles a small bumblebee. The female lays eggs on leaves and necks of bulbs; when the eggs hatch, the young grubs eat their way into the bulbs, opening the way for rot organisms. See page 94 for controls.

Established clumps need dividing only when flower production and bloom quality decline. It's easiest to dig and divide clumps (or transplant them to another location) just after foliage dies down, when you can still see where plants are. Replant bulbs within a month of digging.

Container culture. General directions "B" on page 91 outline basic container culture. To force *Narcissus* for earlier bloom, see pages 92 and 93 for different methods.

NERINE
Photo on page 67

Type of bulb: True bulb

Season of bloom: Autumn

Colors: Red, orange, pink, white

Grows to: 1½ to 2 feet

When to plant: Late summer, early autumn

Where to plant: Sun; part shade where summers are hot

How deep to plant: Top of bulb neck just above soil surface

Hardiness: Varies (see below); in regions beyond hardiness limits, grow as container plants

These are South African relatives of the spider lily (*Lycoris*), which they closely resemble. The most popular species have strap-shaped leaves that usually complete their growth and die back before the bloom period, then reappear after flowering ends. The broad funnel-shaped flowers appear in clusters atop smooth stems; each has six spreading segments, recurved at the tips.

The hardiest species (to 10°F/ −12°C) is *N. bowdenii*. Its 2-foot stems carry clusters of eight to twelve 3-inch-long flowers. Blossoms are typically soft pink with a deeper pink stripe down the center of each segment, but bulb specialists may also offer forms with deeper pink to red blooms. The inch-wide leaves may reach 1 foot long; they die down in late spring or early summer, then reappear shortly before or during the bloom period.

The Guernsey lily, *N. sarniensis*, is similar to *N. bowdenii* in size

and height. It's not as hardy, though, surviving only to about 20°F/ − 7°C. The species has flowers of iridescent crimson, but its forms and hybrids bear blossoms in a wider range of colors: pink, coral, orange, scarlet, and white, usually with a silvery or golden sheen. Foot-long, strap-shaped leaves begin growth after the blooming period ends.

Prominently extended stamens (as in *Lycoris*) distinguish the gold-dusted scarlet blossoms of *N. curvifolia* 'Fothergillii Major' (hardy to 20°F/ − 7°C). The bloom clusters are carried on 1½-foot stems; strap-shaped leaves up to a foot long develop after flowering finishes.

N. filifolia and *N. masonorum* differ from the three species just described in their evergreen, almost grasslike foliage. *N. filifolia*'s foot-tall stems bear clusters of four to twelve narrow-segmented, rose red blossoms, each just 1 inch long. *N. masonorum* looks much the same, but it's shorter and produces fewer blossoms per stem. Both species are hardy to 20°F/ − 7°C.

Uses. Like *Lycoris*, *Nerine* provides a bright color accent among plantings of perennials or shrubs that tolerate (or require) dry soil in summer. It's also an excellent container plant.

Garden culture. *Nerine* needs well-drained soil, preferably sandy rather than claylike. Where summers are hot and dry, choose a planting area in partial shade; elsewhere, plant in full sun.

Set out bulbs 1 foot apart, keeping tops of bulb necks just above soil surface. Water bulbs well after planting, but wait until growth begins before starting regular watering.

When foliage starts to yellow and die down in late spring, cut back on water; after foliage has died back completely, withhold all water and keep soil dry until flower stalks emerge. Then resume a regular watering routine. Leave established clumps undisturbed unless you need to increase or move plantings.

Container culture. All types of *Nerine* can be grown in climates beyond their hardiness limits if planted in containers and overwintered indoors (see *Lycoris*).

ORNITHOGALUM

CHINCHERINCHEE
STAR OF BETHLEHEM

Photo on page 67

Type of bulb: True bulb
Season of bloom: Spring
Colors: White
Grows to: 1 to 2 feet
When to plant: Early autumn
Where to plant: Sun or part shade
How deep to plant: 3 inches
Hardiness: Varies (see below); in regions beyond hardiness limits, grow as container plants

Three species of *Ornithogalum* are readily available. All three bear starlike white blossoms, and two take their common name—star of Bethlehem—from the flower shape.

The hardiest species (to −20°F/ −29°C) is *O. umbellatum,* the star of Bethlehem. This tolerant plant increases rapidly, which can be an asset or a liability: plants quickly spread to fill bare areas, but may naturalize to the point of becoming weedy. Foot-tall stems bear loose clusters of inch-wide white flowers; the back of each narrow petal is striped green. Grasslike leaves are about as long as the flower stems.

Fragrant *O. arabicum,* known as Arabian star of Bethlehem, has the most striking blooms: broad-petaled, 2-inch blossoms of purest white, each centered with a shiny, beadlike black pistil. Blossom clusters are carried on 2-foot stems; bluish green, strap-shaped leaves may reach the same length as the stems, but they're usually floppy rather than upright. *O. arabicum* is hardy to 0°F/−18°C and performs best where summers are warm and dry.

O. thyrsoides, commonly called chincherinchee, produces elongated clusters of 2-inch flowers with brownish green centers. Stems grow 1½ to 2 feet tall; upright, bright green 2-inch-wide leaves are shorter than the stems (to just 1 foot) and usually start to die back while flowering is in progress. Like *O. arabicum,* this species is hardy to 0°F/−18°C. However, gardeners in colder regions may be able to grow it

outdoors by planting against a southwest-facing wall and applying a winter mulch (see page 89) after the first frost.

Uses. Naturalizing is the best use for *O. umbellatum,* but *O. arabicum* and *O. thyrsoides* make attractive accents among annuals and perennials. Foliage of the latter two species dies down during or after the bloom season, so locate them where other plants will conceal the withering leaves.

Garden culture. Choose a planting area with well-drained soil, and dig in plenty of organic matter prior to planting. Then set in bulbs, 3 inches deep and 3 to 4 inches apart. *O. umbellatum* and *O. thyrsoides* will take regular watering all year round; *O. arabicum* needs moisture during autumn, winter, and spring, but requires dry, warm (or hot) summer conditions in order to form flower buds for the following year.

Dig and divide plantings only when a decline in vigor and bloom quality signals that clumps have become overcrowded.

Container culture. For *O. arabicum* and *O. thyrsoides,* follow directions "C" on page 91.

OXALIS

Photo on page 67

Type of bulb: True bulb for species discussed here
Season of bloom: Spring, summer, autumn, winter
Colors: Lavender, pink, yellow, white, red
Grows to: 4 to 12 inches
When to plant: Late summer or autumn
Where to plant: Sun; filtered sun or light shade where summers are hot
How deep to plant: 1 inch
Hardiness: Varies (see below); in regions beyond hardiness limits, grow as container plants

Gardeners familiar only with the weedy, invasive *Oxalis* species will find the following attractive, well-

mannered bulbous kinds a pleasant surprise. (Other *Oxalis* species may grow from rhizomes or tubers.) All species described below bear five-petaled flowers with a broad funnel shape and feature foliage that resembles clover.

O. adenophylla (hardy to −10°F/ −23°C) forms a dense tuft of foliage just 4 inches tall. Each gray-green leaf is divided into 12 to 22 crinkly leaflets. Four to six-inch-tall stems appear in late spring; each bears up to three 1-inch-wide lavender-pink blossoms, centered and veined with deeper lavender.

Summer-blooming *O. bowiei* (hardy to 0°F/−18°C) has downy, cloverlike, 2-inch leaves and foot-tall stems topped with clusters of three to twelve pink to rosy purple 2-inch flowers. *O. deppei* (hardy to 20°F/−7°C) bears clusters of red or white flowers in spring, but it's grown primarily as a foliage plant. Each 2-inch-wide leaf looks like a four-leaf clover with maroon staining on the lower third of the leaflets.

Two other good-looking *Oxalis* species are *O. hirta* and *O. purpurea,* both hardy to about 20°F/−7°C. *O. hirta*'s flexible, branching stems eventually become trailing with the weight of their small, cloverlike, gray-green leaves. Inch-wide rose-pink flowers appear in late autumn and winter. Blossoming at the same time is *O. purpurea.* Its large, cloverlike leaves grow in clumps up to 5 inches tall; yellow-throated flowers of white, lavender, or rose-pink are carried just above the foliage mass. For the largest flowers (up to 2 inches across), look for forms sold as 'Grand Duchess'.

Uses. *Oxalis* is attractive in rock gardens and along partly shaded walkways; all types are good container subjects.

Garden culture. Plant bulbs 1 inch deep, 6 inches apart, in good, well-drained soil amended with plenty of organic matter before planting. Filtered sunlight or light shade is preferable in hot-summer regions, but plants appreciate full sun where summers are cool to mild (or overcast). Water all types of *Oxalis* regularly during the growth and flowering season. After bloom finishes, water sparingly until new growth resumes several months later. Divide infrequently, only when you need to move or increase plantings.

Container culture. Follow directions "A" on page 91. If you're growing plants indoors, place them in a window that receives morning sunlight. Use the watering regime outlined for in-ground plantings, leaving bulbs in their containers during the nearly dry dormant period that follows flowering. Fertilize monthly with a liquid fertilizer during the growth and flowering period.

POLIANTHES tuberosa

TUBEROSE

Photo on page 67

Type of bulb: Rhizome (with bulb-like top)
Season of bloom: Summer, early autumn
Color: White
Grows to: 2½ to 3½ feet
When to plant: Spring
Where to plant: Sun
How deep to plant: 2 inches
Hardiness: To about 20°F/−7°C; in colder regions, dig and store over winter as for *Begonia* or grow as a container plant

The intense fragrance of tuberoses is legendary. These plants were popular with home gardeners around the turn of the century, but today they're primarily grown by the French perfume industry.

Each rhizome produces a fountain of narrow, grasslike leaves about 1½ feet tall. Flower spikes rise above the foliage, producing loose whorls of outward-facing blossoms in summer or early autumn. The tallest tuberose (to 3½ feet) is the form sometimes sold as 'Mexican Single'; it bears trumpet-shaped single blooms about 2½ inches long. But the most widely sold variety is double-flowered 'The Pearl', which reaches a height of about 2½ feet.

In order to bloom year after year, tuberoses need a long warm season (at least 4 months) before flowering.

Where this can be provided outdoors, you can plant rhizomes directly in the ground; elsewhere, grow them in containers.

Uses. Though tuberoses are attractive in foliage and flower, they're primarily valued for their fragrance. Locate plants where both looks and scent can be appreciated: in mixed border plantings, for example, or in containers on patio, terrace, or deck.

Garden culture. Choose a sunny spot with well-drained soil; then amend soil with a generous amount of organic matter prior to planting. Check rhizomes to make sure they're healthy: if they're alive and well, they'll show signs of green at the growing tips.

Set rhizomes 2 inches deep, 4 to 6 inches apart, and water enough to moisten the planting area. As soon as leaves appear, begin regular watering—plants need plenty of moisture during the growing and flowering season. If soil or water is alkaline, apply an acid fertilizer when growth begins.

When foliage starts to yellow in autumn, withhold water and let soil go dry. Where winter temperatures remain above 20°F/−7°C, rhizomes may stay in the ground. However, many gardeners in these areas (and all those living in colder regions) prefer to store rhizomes indoors over the winter. Dig plants after leaves have yellowed; cut off dead leaves, let rhizomes dry for 2 weeks, and store over winter as for *Begonia*.

Container culture. In regions where the growing season is shorter than 4 months, start rhizomes in pots indoors, keeping them in a spot where the temperature remains above 60°F/16°C. Plant one or two rhizomes in an 8-inch container, using the soil mix described under "A" on page 91. Water thoroughly after planting, but wait until leaves emerge to begin regular watering. As soon as night temperatures reliably remain above 60°F/16°C, you can move growing plants outdoors; keep them in containers for portable display, or carefully transplant into garden flower beds. Give container plants monthly applications of a liquid fertilizer until flowering begins.

PUSCHKINIA scilloides

Photo on page 67

Type of bulb: True bulb
Season of bloom: Early spring
Colors: Blue, white
Grows to: 6 inches
When to plant: Autumn; mid to late summer (from divisions)
Where to plant: Sun or light shade
How deep to plant: 3 inches
Hardiness: To about −40°F/−40°C; needs some subfreezing winter temperatures

One herald of the springtime is this stocky relative of the better known bluebells (*Endymion*) and squills (*Scilla*). Each bulb produces two broad, strap-shaped, upright leaves and a slightly taller flower spike bearing up to 20 six-petaled blossoms. Blooms are roughly star shaped and about an inch wide; the usual color is light blue, but white-flowered forms are also sold. All flowers have a greenish blue stripe down the center of each petal.

For best performance, this plant needs cold winter weather, with some subfreezing night temperatures.

Uses. *Puschkinia* is a good choice for naturalizing and for rock garden plantings. Naturalize bulbs in grassy patches, or plant in drifts under deciduous trees, along pathways, or in front of shrub borders.

Garden culture. Set bulbs 3 inches deep in well-drained soil; for a massed effect, space them about 3 inches apart. After planting, give bulbs one thorough watering to settle soil and initiate root growth. Keep soil just slightly moist until foliage appears; then water regularly until leaves start to yellow in early summer. During the summer dormant period, plants need very little water.

Established plantings seldom need dividing to relieve overcrowding. However, you can dig bulbs as needed to increase a planting or start new ones; do so in mid to late summer and replant right away.

Container culture. Follow directions "B" on page 91.

RANUNCULUS asiaticus

Photos on pages 11 and 67

Type of bulb: Tuberous root
Season of bloom: Spring
Colors: Pink, red, orange, yellow, cream, white, multicolors
Grows to: 1½ to 2 feet
When to plant: Autumn; spring where winter temperatures fall below 10°F/−12°C
Where to plant: Sun
How deep to plant: 1 to 2 inches
Hardiness: To about 10°F/−12°C; in colder regions, dig and store over winter as for *Begonia*

It's surprising that *Ranunculus* has never acquired the common name "magic flower"—the production of showy blossoms from such a small, peculiar-looking root is the equal of any conjurer's trick. The bright flowers—3 to 5 inches wide, semidouble to fully double—have been variously (and accurately) described as resembling small peonies, camellias, and artificial crêpe-paper flowers. One to four blooms are carried on each 1½ to 2-foot stem. Plants are full foliaged, with dark green, finely divided leaves; when not yet in bloom, they look much like bunches of flat-leaf parsley.

The most widely sold type of ranunculus is the Tecolote strain, which includes all the colors listed above as well as pastel shades edged in darker, contrasting hues. Nurseries offer tuberous roots of various sizes; both small and large roots produce equally large blossoms, but the larger ones produce a greater number of flowers.

Uses. Ranunculus fills a number of roles in the garden. You can set out plants in solid beds, use them in drifts of single or mixed colors, or spot them as accent clumps in mixed plantings of annuals and perennials. Container culture is a possibility, too. In mild-winter areas, ranunculus is a successful alternative to tulips for landscape work.

Garden culture. Where tuberous roots are hardy in the ground, autumn is the time to plant. The sooner you set out roots, the earlier they'll bloom, so plant earliest where spring comes first—as early as October in low desert and other areas where mild, springlike weather arrives during the winter months.

In regions too cold for tuberous roots to overwinter outdoors, plant them in spring for bloom from late spring into early summer (hot weather terminates flower production). If you live in a cold-winter region, you'll get the longest possible flowering season by starting roots indoors 6 weeks to 1 month before the normal last-frost date. Plant them in pots or flats, using either of the soil mixes described in "B" on page 91.

Ranunculus needs well-drained soil, liberally amended with organic matter prior to planting. In clay and other heavy soils, plant in raised beds to promote good drainage, and set tuberous roots no deeper than 1 inch. (In lighter soils, they can be planted about 2 inches deep.) Position tuberous roots with the "prongs" facing down, spacing them 6 to 8 inches apart. Water the soil thoroughly after planting, but don't water again until the leaves emerge.

Birds are very fond of ranunculus shoots, so you may need to protect sprouting plants with netting or wire. Another solution to the problem is to start plants in pots or flats (see above), then set them out in the garden when they're 4 to 6 inches tall—too mature to appeal to birds.

While plants are flowering, remove faded blossoms so plants will continue to bloom rather than diverting their energy to seed production.

As the weather grows warmer, flowering will cease and foliage will begin to yellow. At this point, stop watering and let foliage die back. Where tuberous roots are hardy in the ground, you may leave them undisturbed—provided that soil can be kept dry throughout the summer. However, most gardeners in all regions dig plants when foliage yellows and cut off the tops, then let the roots dry for a week or two and store them as for *Begonia* until planting time.

Container culture. Follow directions "B" on page 91.

SCHIZOSTYLIS coccinea

CRIMSON FLAG
KAFFIR LILY
Photo on page 70

Type of bulb: Rhizome
Season of bloom: Midautumn
Colors: Red, pink
Grows to: 1½ to 2 feet
When to plant: Spring
Where to plant: Sun to light shade
How deep to plant: ½ to 1 inch
Hardiness: To about 10°F/−12°C; in colder regions, grow as a container plant
NOTE: *Clivia miniata* is also called "Kaffir lily."

Like *Gladiolus,* crimson flag has upright, swordlike leaves and a spike of closely set flowers; the starlike 2-inch blossoms, however, recall another relative, *Watsonia*.

"Bright" is the word for this plant's flowers, and as the common name indicates, bright crimson is the color of the basic species. The variety 'Mrs. Hegarty' has rose-pink blossoms. Either color is a particular standout in midautumn, a time of year when few other flowers are making a major display.

Uses. See *Gladiolus*.

Garden culture. In its native South Africa, crimson flag grows in highly organic soil that's moist but well aerated. Dig generous amounts of peat moss and other organic matter into the planting area; then set out rhizomes, ½ to 1 inch deep and 1 foot apart. Water generously from planting time until the flowering period ends; then water sparingly until growth resumes the following spring. If clumps become crowded, dig in early spring, separate so that each division has at least five shoots, and replant.

Container culture. Follow directions "B" on page 91. In climates where winter lows dip below 10°F/−12°C, overwinter container-grown crimson flag in a sunny room that's cool at night (45° to 55°F/7° to 13°C), up to 70°F/21°C during the day.

Ranunculus asiaticus

Puschkinia scilloides

Polianthes tuberosa

Nerine sarniensis

Oxalis bowiei

Ornithogalum arabicum

SCILLA

SQUILL

Photo on page 70

Type of bulb: True bulb
Season of bloom: Winter, spring
Colors: Blue, violet, lilac pink, white
Grows to: 3 to 12 inches
When to plant: Autumn; summer or early autumn (from divisions)
Where to plant: Sun during bloom time, part shade during rest of year
How deep to plant: 2 to 4 inches, depending on species
Hardiness: Varies (see below)
NOTE: For two plants once classed as *Scilla*—English bluebell and Spanish bluebell—see *Endymion*.

Gardeners in cold-winter climates know *Scilla* as one of the harbingers of spring: two of its species often coincide in bloom with winter aconite (*Eranthis hyemalis*) and snowdrop (*Galanthus*).

All types of *Scilla* have bell-shaped or starlike flowers, borne on leafless stems that rise from clumps of strap-shaped leaves. Among the earliest to flower is 8-inch-tall *S. bifolia*; as the specific name implies, each bulb usually produces just two leaves. The starlike blossoms, carried three to eight to each flowering stem, are suspended by short, threadlike stalks. A vivid, almost turquoise shade of blue is the most common color, but you may also find forms with flowers of white, violet blue, or light pink. *S. bifolia* is hardy to $-30°F/-35°C$ and requires some subfreezing winter temperatures for good performance.

Two other early-flowering species are *S. siberica* (Siberian squill) and *S. tubergeniana*. Like *S. bifolia*, these are hardy to $-30°F/-35°C$ and demand some winter chilling. *S. tubergeniana* bears nodding clusters of three or four pale blue, starlike blossoms on stems to 6 inches tall; a darker blue stripe runs down the center of each flower segment. *S. siberica*'s typical color is an intense medium blue; several six-segmented flowers shaped like flaring bells hang from each 3 to 6-inch stem. Varieties of this species bloom in white, lilac pink, and light to dark shades of violet blue, often with a darker stripe down each segment's center. 'Spring Beauty' has brilliant violet blue blooms, larger than those of the species.

Differing in hardiness and appearance is *S. peruviana*—commonly called Peruvian scilla, though it's native to Mediterranean Europe. Its large bulbs produce numerous rather floppy leaves; 10 to 12-inch stems rise from the foliage clumps, each topped with a dome-shaped cluster of 50 or more starlike flowers. Most forms of this species have bluish purple blooms, but a white-flowered variety is sometimes available. *S. peruviana* is hardy only to $20°F/-7°C$ and performs well in regions with little or no winter chill.

Uses. Naturalizing is the best use for the hardier species; try them in small patches, larger drifts, or as part of a "carpet" of various plants and flowers. Plant them under deciduous shrubs or trees; meadows and fields are also good locations, as long as they're in part or light shade during summer.

Peruvian scilla may also be naturalized, but it's a bit coarse textured for wildflower-style plantings. Try it in clumps along pathways, at edges of mixed plantings, or in containers.

Garden culture. All types of *Scilla* appreciate well-drained soil enriched with organic matter before planting. Set the three hardy species 2 to 3 inches deep, about 4 inches apart, but plant bulbs of Peruvian scilla 3 to 4 inches deep and space them about 6 inches apart. Water all species regularly during their growth and bloom period; decrease water when foliage yellows.

Divide plantings only to relieve overcrowding (which will be evidenced by decreased vigor and poorer blossom quality). Peruvian scilla enters a brief dormant period after its leaves wither in summer; dig and replant soon after foliage has died back completely. Other species may be divided in late summer or early autumn.

Container culture. For Peruvian scilla, see directions "C" on page 91.

SINNINGIA speciosa

GLOXINIA

Photo on page 70

Type of bulb: Tuber
Season of bloom: Summer
Colors: Lavender, purple, red, pink, white, blue, multicolors
Grows to: 1 foot
When to plant: Winter or early spring
Where to plant: Bright indirect light
How deep to plant: ½ inch
Hardiness: Tender; store indoors over winter (see below)

"Bold" and "velvety" are two key words for gloxinias. These squat, full-foliaged plants have broad, oval leaves with the look of quilted green velvet; each grows 6 inches long (or longer). Blossoms, clustered near the top of the plant, are ruffled bells up to 4 inches across, all with a velvety sheen. Available colors include white, red, pink, blue, and light to dark shades of purple; in many types, blossoms show combinations of several hues. You'll see dots of darker color on lighter shades, light or white edges on solid colors, and blotches of dark color on light.

Because gloxinias are usually grown in greenhouses or as house plants, many gardeners assume they must be difficult to grow. But it's only their need for warmth that restricts gloxinias to indoor culture even in temperate climates. During their growth and bloom period, they need night temperatures above $65°F/18°C$, and even while dormant they should be kept around $60°F/16°C$.

Container culture. For each tuber, choose a container large enough to leave 2 inches between all sides of the tuber and the container edges. Fill containers with a soil mix of equal parts peat moss, perlite, and leaf mold or compost; then set in tubers ½ inch deep.

Place containers in a warm location (about $72°F/22°C$ during the day, no lower than $65°F/18°C$ at night) where they'll receive plenty of bright light but no direct sun. Water sparingly until the first leaves appear, then increase watering as roots and leaves grow. Apply water to the soil only, or pour it into containers' drip saucers and let it be absorbed by capillary action. (Be sure to pour off any water unabsorbed after an hour.) From the time leaves emerge until flowers fade, apply a liquid fertilizer diluted to half strength every 2 weeks.

After flowering ceases, gradually withhold water and let foliage wither. When leaves have died down entirely, plants are completely dormant; at this point, move containers to a darkened spot where temperatures will remain around 60°F/16°C. Moisten soil just often enough to keep tubers from shriveling.

When tubers show signs of resuming growth in midwinter, repot in fresh soil mix. If you see that roots have filled a container, move the tuber to a container that's 1 to 2 inches wider; leaf and flower size decrease when plants become potbound.

SPARAXIS tricolor

HARLEQUIN FLOWER

Photo on page 70

Type of bulb: Corm
Season of bloom: Late spring
Colors: Yellow, orange, red, pink, purple, white
Grows to: 15 inches
When to plant: Autumn; early spring where winter temperatures fall below 20°F/ − 7°C
Where to plant: Sun
How deep to plant: 2 inches
Hardiness: To about 20°F/ − 7°C; in colder regions, dig and store over winter as for *Gladiolus*

One look at its bright blossoms explains why *Sparaxis* is commonly called "harlequin flower." Each bloom has a patchwork arrangement of colors: one color in its chalicelike center, another color surrounding this, and still another on the balance of the spreading petals. Flowers are up to 2 inches across, borne in loose spikes on slender stems that rise from fans of swordlike leaves.

Uses. *Sparaxis* looks best when planted in groups—as an accent in borders or along pathways. For a brilliant tapestrylike effect, naturalize corms in a sunny garden spot.

Garden culture. Well-drained soil in a sunny spot suits *Sparaxis*. Plant corms 2 inches deep, 3 to 4 inches apart—in autumn where corms are hardy in the ground, in early spring in colder regions. Water regularly during the growing period. Withhold water when leaves yellow; keep soil dry during summer.

Where corms are hardy in the ground (and summers are dry), you can leave plantings undisturbed for a number of years. In colder regions with dry summers, dig corms in late summer and store over winter as for *Gladiolus*. In all moist-summer regions, grow *Sparaxis* as a container plant so you can provide dry summer dormancy.

Container culture. Follow directions "B" on page 91.

SPREKELIA formosissima

AZTEC LILY
JACOBEAN LILY
ST. JAMES LILY

Photo on page 70

Type of bulb: True bulb
Season of bloom: Primarily early summer
Color: Red
Grows to: 1 to 1½ feet
When to plant: Autumn; spring where winter temperatures fall below 20°F/ − 7°C
Where to plant: Sun
How deep to plant: 3 to 4 inches
Hardiness: To about 20°F/ − 7°C; in colder regions, dig and store over winter as for *Dahlia*

Aztec lily's linear foliage is reminiscent of daffodil leaves, but wait till you see the flowers! The irregularly shaped dark red blossoms have understandably been likened to orchids. Each stem bears one 6-inch flower; display increases if plants are left undisturbed for several years

to form clumps in the ground or containers. In climates with little or no frost, plants may bloom several times a year if you give them a dry period after blossoming, then resume regular watering to trigger a new growth cycle.

Uses. Aztec lily is a striking flower and foliage accent in the summer garden. Plant it in clumps at the foreground of mixed annual and perennial beds, or grow it in containers.

Garden culture. Plant bulbs 3 to 4 inches deep and about 8 inches apart in good, well-drained soil—in autumn where bulbs are hardy in the ground, in spring in colder regions. Water regularly from the time growth begins until bloom finishes. In frost-free areas, let plants go dry for several weeks after flowers fade; then resume regular watering to initiate another bloom period.

Where bulbs can stay in the ground over winter, you can leave plantings undisturbed for many years. When vigor and bloom quality decline, dig, separate, and replant bulbs in autumn. In cold-winter regions, dig bulbs in autumn before the first frost; dry them with foliage attached, then store over winter as for *Begonia*.

Container culture. Follow the directions outlined for *Hippeastrum*, but keep temperatures about five degrees lower during the growing and flowering period.

STERNBERGIA lutea

Photo on page 70

Type of bulb: True bulb
Season of bloom: Autumn
Color: Yellow
Grows to: 4 to 9 inches
When to plant: Mid to late summer
Where to plant: Sun
How deep to plant: 4 inches
Hardiness: To about 20°F/ − 7°C; to about − 10°F/ − 23°C with winter protection (see page 89)

An ideal choice for the impatient gardener, *Sternbergia* offers almost
(Continued on page 71)

Schizostylis coccinea

Scilla peruviana

Sinningia *hybrid*

Sprekelia formosissima

Tigridia pavonia

Sternbergia lutea

Sparaxis tricolor

instant gratification: bulbs planted in mid to late summer burst into bloom in early autumn. Each bulb produces a single flower that looks something like a bright yellow crocus—about 1½ inches long, chalice shaped at first, then opening out to a wide star. Narrow, linear leaves appear at the same time as blossoms and eventually grow up to 1 foot long. They persist through the winter, then die back in spring.

Uses. Plant *Sternbergia* in rock gardens or pockets in paved patios, along pathways, or in containers.

Garden culture. Plant bulbs as soon as they're available. Choose a sunny spot with well-drained soil, preferably in an area that receives little or no watering during early summer. Plant bulbs about 6 inches apart and 4 inches deep. Water regularly from planting time until the bloom period ends, then withhold water; after flowering, natural moisture from winter and spring rain or snow should carry plants through to their next dormant time.

Where winter temperatures drop to 20°F/−7°C or lower, give plantings winter protection as described on page 89. Clumps increase in beauty as bulbs multiply, so dig and separate (in August) only when vigor and flower quality decline.

Container culture. Follow directions "B" on page 91.

TIGRIDIA pavonia

MEXICAN SHELL FLOWER
TIGER FLOWER

Photo on page 70

Type of bulb: True bulb
Season of bloom: Summer
Colors: Red, orange, yellow, pink, cream, white
Grows to: 1½ to 2½ feet
When to plant: Spring
Where to plant: Sun; part shade where summers are hot
How deep to plant: 2 to 4 inches
Hardiness: To about 0°F/−18°C; in colder regions, dig and store over winter as for *Gladiolus*

The hot, flashy colors of *Tigridia*'s blossoms are appropriate for its summertime bloom season. The bright flowers are triangular, up to 6 inches across; each consists of three large outer segments and three smaller inner ones. The chalicelike blossom center is usually boldly spotted with a contrasting color—only the Immaculata strain is spotless.

An individual flower lasts just one day, but since each stem carries a number of buds, the blooming period lasts for several weeks. Flower stems are upright and branching, rising from fans of narrow, swordlike, ribbed leaves up to 1½ feet long.

Uses. *Tigridia* adds a dominant splash of color wherever it's placed: in clumps, in a border of summer flowers, or in containers.

Garden culture. Plant *Tigridia* bulbs in spring after weather warms up (nighttime temperatures must not fall below 60°F/16°C). Choose a spot in full sun if summer heat is not intense; in hot-summer regions, plants appreciate afternoon shade. Set bulbs 2 to 4 inches deep, 4 to 8 inches apart, in well-drained soil. Water regularly throughout the growing and blooming period, then cease watering when foliage yellows. For top performance, apply a timed-release fertilizer once, when bulbs break ground; or give bimonthly applications of a liquid fertilizer diluted to half strength, starting when leaves emerge and stopping when blossoms open.

Where bulbs are hardy in the ground, you can leave plantings undisturbed for 3 or 4 years before dividing. Dig bulbs after foliage dies back in autumn and store over winter as for *Gladiolus*; wait until spring planting time to separate bulbs from each other.

Spider mites are the principal problem for Tigridia, detectable by the yellowish or whitish streaks they leave on foliage. Begin applying controls (see page 94) when leaves are several inches high. Gophers are another pest; they're fond of the bulbs. See page 95 for controls.

Container culture. Follow directions "B" on page 91.

TRITONIA

FLAME FREESIA

Photo on page 75

Type of bulb: Corm
Season of bloom: Late spring
Colors: Pink, red, orange, yellow, white
Grows to: 10 to 18 inches
When to plant: Early autumn; spring where winter temperatures fall below 20°F/−7°C
Where to plant: Sun
How deep to plant: 2 to 3 inches
Hardiness: To about 20°F/−7°C; in colder regions, dig and store over winter as for *Gladiolus*

Fans of swordlike leaves and branched spikes of bright, broad, funnel-shaped flowers mark *Tritonia* as a close relative of *Ixia*, *Crocosmia*, *Freesia*, and *Sparaxis*. And in fact the most commonly sold species, *T. crocata,* is often called "flame freesia." The variety *T.c. miniata* has bright red flowers, while 'Princess Beatrix' is a stunning deep orange. Occasionally, you'll find other varieties in white, yellow, and shades of pink. *T. crocata* and its varieties have broad-petaled blossoms up to 2 inches across, borne on branching spikes to 1½ feet tall; flowers are arranged alternately on either side of the stem.

T. hyalina, the other commonly sold species, grows to about 1 foot tall; its orange flowers have narrower petals than those of *T. crocata,* with a transparent area near the base of each petal.

Uses. Grow *Tritonia* in clumps or drifts, as a colorful accent in the foreground of plantings that require little watering during summer.

Garden culture. Like its close relatives, *Tritonia* needs well-drained soil in a sunny location, regular watering during growing and flowering time, and little or no moisture after foliage starts to yellow. Plant corms 2 to 3 inches deep, 3 inches apart. In dry-summer areas where winter temperatures remain above 20°F/−7°C, plant in early autumn; dig and divide only when plantings become crowded and vigor and bloom quality decline. In colder regions where summers are dry, plant in spring; dig corms in late summer or early autumn and store over winter as for *Gladiolus*. In all moist-summer regions, grow *Tritonia* in containers so you can give corms the dry summer dormancy they need.

Container culture. Follow directions "B" on page 91.

TULBAGHIA
Photo on page 75

Type of bulb: Rhizome
Season of bloom: Spring, summer, autumn, winter
Color: Pinkish lavender
Grows to: 1 to 2 feet
When to plant: Any time of year
Where to plant: Sun
How deep to plant: Just beneath soil surface
Hardiness: To about 20°F/−7°C; in colder regions, grow as a container plant

One general description covers both available species of *Tulbaghia*: dense clumps of narrow, linear leaves send up slim stems topped by clusters of small, trumpet-shaped, pinkish lavender flowers. *T. fragrans* has 1-inch-wide gray-green leaves that grow up to 1 foot tall; clusters of 20 to 30 flowers appear in winter or early spring.

T. violacea's leaves are bluish green and narrower than those of *T. fragrans,* and it has fewer blossoms per cluster—only 8 to 20. Variety *T.v.* 'Silver Lace' has leaves rimmed in white, with a hairline tint of lavender at the edges. This species blooms most heavily in spring and summer. *T. violacea* bears the common name "society garlic," and for good reason: leaves and flower stems give off an oniony or garlicky odor when bruised or crushed. You can even use the leaves in cooking.

Uses. Use *Tulbaghia* at the foreground in mixed borders of annuals and perennials; it's also attractive in containers.

Garden culture. Amenable *Tulbaghia* will grow in light or heavy soil, though it does best in well-drained soil liberally amended with organic matter before planting. Plant at any time of year, from containers or divisions, in a sunny spot; give plants regular watering for best performance. Divide clumps whenever you want to increase the planting area or when foliage and flower quality decline. (Where summers are hot, early spring and early autumn are the best times to divide.)

Container culture. Follow directions "C" on page 91. Where winter temperatures fall below 20°F/−7°C, move potted plants indoors at the first signs of frost; overwinter in a sunny window in a cool room (maximum temperature of 60°F/16°C).

TULIPA
TULIP
Photos on pages 6 and 75

Type of bulb: True bulb
Season of bloom: Spring
Colors: Purple, red, pink, lavender, white, buff, cream, yellow, orange, bronze, mauve, maroon, multicolors
Grows to: 6 inches to over 3 feet
When to plant: Autumn; winter in mildest regions
Where to plant: Sun or light shade
How deep to plant: Varies depending on size of bulb
Hardiness: To about −40°F/−40°C; almost all need some subfreezing winter temperatures

To many people—especially those living in cold-winter regions—tulips and daffodils signify spring. But while daffodils may be strewn about with naturalistic abandon, tulips are generally thought of as orderly flowers: neatly planted in garden beds, in serried ranks of even height. In fact, many types of tulips are rather rigidly formal, but as a group, these plants vary considerably in height, form, color, and general character. Some are quite bizarre (the "broken" kinds and parrot varieties); some of the short types and

many of the species look like wildflowers; and the double-flowered sorts resemble peonies.

Most of the tulips in modern gardens fit into the classifications established jointly by the Royal Dutch Bulb Growers and the Royal Horticultural Society of England. These groups are based primarily on appearance rather than on strict botanical relationship: all the varieties in each division have the same general flower shape and height range. The first 17 divisions encompass the familiar garden hybrid types; the remainder include various popular species tulips and their hybrids.

Large hybrid tulips

The divisions described below are listed in approximate order of bloom (the last three are fairly new "novelty" hybrid groups, all blooming in late spring).

Single Early tulips. Tulips in this class have large single flowers in red, yellow, or white, on 10 to 16-inch stems. Though they're favorites for growing or forcing indoors in pots, they can also be grown outside, where they bloom from March to mid-April (depending on climate and variety). These tulips aren't adapted to warm-winter climates.

Double Early tulips. Double peony-like flowers—often measuring 4 inches across—grow on 6 to 12-inch stems. Double Early tulips have much the same color range as Single Early types and are often forced for early bloom in containers. They're also effective massed in borders for spring bloom outside; except for a few species tulips, they're usually the first to bloom.

Mendel tulips. Derived from Darwin tulips, Mendel tulips have single blossoms on stems up to 20 inches tall; they bloom later than Single Early and Double Early tulips, but earlier than the Darwins. Colors include red, pink, orange, yellow, and white.

Triumph tulips. Crosses between Single Early tulips and May-flowering types produced the Triumph class: earlier blooming than the Darwins, with heavier, shorter stems (usually not over 20 inches tall). Red, white, yellow, and bi-colored varieties are available.

Darwin tulips. These popular late-flowering tulips are graceful, stately plants with large oval or egg-shaped blooms carried on straight stems to 2½ feet tall. Blossoms are square at the base, but flower segments are typically rounded at the tips. There's a remarkably extensive range of clear, beautiful colors: white, yellow, orange, pink, red, mauve, lilac, purple, and maroon.

Darwin Hybrids. *T. fosterana* and the Darwins are parents of these hybrids. Huge, shining, brilliant flowers show the influence of *T. fosterana;* 2-foot stems recall the Darwin parent. Colors include red and orange; bloom is later than *T. fosterana,* but earlier than Darwins.

Breeder tulips. Large oval or globular flowers are borne on stems up to 40 inches tall. Colors are quite unusual, with orange, bronze, and purple predominating.

Lily-flowered tulips. Formerly included in the Cottage division, these tulips have graceful, lilylike blooms with recurved, pointed segments. Flowers are longer and narrower than those of the Darwins; colors include white and shades of yellow, pink, and red. Bloom time coincides with that of the Darwin Hybrids.

Cottage tulips. These are descendants of varieties found growing in old gardens in the British Isles, Belgium, and France. In size and height, they resemble the Darwins; flowers are oval or egg shaped, often with pointed segments. Colors include red, purple, yellow, pink, orange, and white.

Rembrandt tulips. These are "broken" Darwin tulips, so called because the background flower color is "broken"—streaked or variegated throughout with different colors.

Bizarre tulips. "Broken" Breeder or Cottage tulips constitute this class. Flowers have a yellow background striped or marked with bronze, brown, maroon, or purple.

Bybloems (Bijbloemens). Like the Bizarre division, these are "broken" Breeder or Cottage tulips, but they have a white background with lilac, rose, or purple markings.

Parrot tulips. This class of May-flowering tulips includes sports (mutations) of solid colored varieties of regular form. Their large, long, deeply fringed and ruffled blooms are striped, feathered, and flamed in various colors. Parrot tulips once had weak, floppy stems, but modern types are stouter and stand up well.

Double Late tulips. As the name implies, this class of tulips—often referred to as Peony-flowered—has double blossoms and blooms late in the season. The extremely large, heavy flowers come in orange, rose, yellow, and white.

Fringed tulips. These are variations from Single Early, Double Early, and Darwin tulips. Edges of flower segments are finely fringed.

Viridiflora tulips. Blossoms are edged in green or colored in blends of green with other hues—white, yellow, rose, red, or buff. Stems grow 10 to 20 inches tall.

Multiflowered tulips. Members of this class grow 20 to 27 inches tall, bearing three to six flowers on each stem. Colors include white, yellow, pink, and red.

Species & species hybrid tulips

In addition to the divisions just described, there are classes covering species and species hybrids. Three of these include varieties and hybrids of *T. fosterana, T. greigii,* and *T. kaufmanniana*—all good plants for mild-winter areas.

T. fosterana. This statuesque early-flowering red tulip has the largest blossoms—to 8 inches across—of any tulip, whether species or hybrid, wild type or selected form. Stems reach a height of 8 to 20 inches.

T. greigii. This outstanding species tulip is noted for its large scarlet blossoms, as well as for its beautifully mottled and marked leaves.

T. kaufmanniana. Called the water-lily tulip, this is one of the loveliest, earliest blooming, and sturdiest of the species tulips, widely used in hybridizing. Blooms (up to 3 inches long) are creamy yellow marked with red on the outside; the flower segments open flat in the sun, revealing a bright yellow center. Varieties are available in other colors.

Smaller species tulips. These are sold chiefly by bulb specialists. They have a simpler, more wildflowerlike charm than their large hybrid relatives. Several species will persist from year to year in warm-winter regions.

T. batalinii. Single soft yellow flowers on 6 to 10-inch stems; linear leaves.

T. clusiana. The graceful lady or candy tulip, with slender, medium-size blooms colored rosy red on the outside, creamy white on the inside. A good permanent tulip for areas with little winter chill. *T. c. chrysantha* is star shaped when open. Outside flower segments are pure rose carmine merging to buff at the base; inside segments are pure butter yellow.

T. eichleri. A striking, sculptured-looking tulip. Each shining scarlet flower has a jet black center outlined with yellow.

T. linifolia. Glossy scarlet flowers with a dark purple basal blotch. A striking companion for yellow *T. batalinii,* which blooms at the same time.

T. praestans. Pure orange-scarlet flowers, often two to four to a stem, contrast beautifully with pale green leaves edged with dark red.

T. tarda (T. dasystemon). An appealing little tulip, with clusters of as many as four flowers on each 3 to 5-inch stem. The star-shaped white flowers have prominent yellow centers.

Uses

Rows of tulips look stiff and artificial, as though plants and flowers were made of plastic. Large hybrid types really shine when planted in masses or drifts; they also make bright clumps among other spring-flowering plants, especially lower growing annuals and perennials.

(Continued on next page)

The small species tulips are good choices for rock gardens and mixed plantings, and also naturalize easily where climate permits.

Garden culture

In their native lands, tulip species are accustomed to cold winters (often long and severe), short springs, and hot summers. Except for certain species, most are short-lived in mild-winter regions, even if summers are hot: winter chill is critical for permanence. Nonetheless, gardeners in the South and Southwest can still enjoy tulips each spring if they grow them as annuals, planting new bulbs each year and discarding them after bloom is finished. In these mild regions, store dormant bulbs at 40°F/4°C until November, December, or early January; then plant them 6 to 8 inches deep. The later planting time and greater planting depth ensure that bulbs will be surrounded by cool soil, which they require to root well.

In colder regions—where winter temperatures drop below 32°F/0°C—plant bulbs in early to mid autumn after the soil has cooled.

Tulips need sunshine at least while they're in bloom; stems will lean toward the source of light if the planting area is partly shaded. It's fine to plant bulbs under deciduous trees if the trees won't leaf out until after the blooming season ends. Well-drained soil is another requirement, though the particular type isn't important—both light and heavy soils are satisfactory. Be sure, though, to add plenty of organic matter prior to planting.

Set bulbs two and one-half times as deep as they're wide (except in mild-winter regions—see above); space them 4 to 8 inches apart, depending on the eventual size of the plant. Tulips need plenty of moisture during the growth and flowering period, but can get by with less after foliage dies back.

Gophers and field mice are extraordinarily fond of tulip bulbs. See "Foiling the spoilers" (page 85) and "Rodents" (page 95) for controls. Protect plants from aphids (page 94) during the growing season, particularly if your planting contains any of the "broken" tulips. (The "broken" patterning results from a virus that's spread in part by aphids.)

Large hybrid tulips left in the ground from year to year may or may not perform to your satisfaction. Bloom display tends to be less uniform as plantings increase, because flowers arise from bulbs of various sizes. To keep bulbs (and the blooms they produce) as large as possible, plant them 6 to 8 inches deep. Deep planting slows the rate of increase so that energy is directed toward producing tall stems and big blooms the following season. Also be sure to remove spent flowers so no energy is diverted to seed setting.

If tulips persist in vigor from year to year, they'll eventually need separating. Dig and divide bulbs in late summer; replant at the best time for your area.

Species tulips are a different proposition from most of the larger hybrid types. Most are candidates for rock gardens and for the foreground of mixed plantings; they may be left undisturbed for many years. Dig and separate species tulips (in late summer) whenever they become crowded, or when you need bulbs for planting elsewhere. Replant at the best time for your climate.

Container culture

Refer to directions "B" on page 91 for basic container culture. To force tulips for earlier bloom, see page 92.

VALLOTA speciosa
SCARBOROUGH LILY

Type of bulb: True bulb

Season of bloom: Summer, early autumn

Colors: Orange-red, white, pink

Grows to: 2 feet

When to plant: Early summer; or autumn, just after flowering

Where to plant: Light shade; sun where summers are cool and overcast

How deep to plant: Just beneath soil surface

Hardiness: To about 25°F/−4°C

Scarborough lily looks much like a more delicate version of its close relative the Dutch amaryllis (*Hippeastrum*). Each thick flower stalk is topped with a cluster of up to 10 broad, funnel-shaped blossoms; the typical color is orange-red, but you'll sometimes find white or pink-flowered forms. The glossy evergreen leaves, strap shaped and 1 to 2 feet long, are attractive throughout the year.

Where winters are very mild, Scarborough lily can be planted in the ground. But most gardeners, even those living within the hardiness range, prefer to grow this plant in containers.

Uses. Outdoors, Scarborough lily is attractive for individual accent clumps or limited-area ground cover plantings. Use container-grown plants for accents indoors or on patio, deck, or terrace.

Garden culture. Select a location receiving plenty of bright, indirect light—in light shade under deciduous trees, for example (bulbs will almost always survive competition from tree roots). Except where summers are cool and overcast, don't choose a direct-sun planting area. Plant bulbs in well-drained soil enriched with organic matter prior to planting, setting them 1 to 1½ feet apart and positioning tips just beneath the soil surface. Water regularly during summer and throughout the flowering season; give less water during the winter-and-spring dormant period, but never let soil go completely dry.

Divide clumps infrequently, only when overcrowding causes a decline in vigor and bloom quality. Small bulbs will eventually form around the larger bulbs. To increase your planting, remove these in summer before bloom and plant separately.

Container culture. Follow general directions for *Hippeastrum*. Plant bulbs in early summer; throughout the growth and flowering period, water regularly and apply a liquid fertilizer monthly. During winter and spring, keep soil just barely moist and don't fertilize at all. Resume regular watering and fertilizing when growth begins in early summer.

Veltheimia viridifolia

Tulbaghia violacea

Watsonia pyramidata

Zephyranthes grandiflora

Tritonia crocata

Tulipa clusiana chrysantha

Zantedeschia rehmannii *hybrids*

75

VELTHEIMIA viridifolia

Photo on page 75

Type of bulb: True bulb
Season of bloom: Winter, early spring
Colors: Pink with green
Grows to: 12 to 15 inches
When to plant: Autumn
Where to plant: Filtered sun, part shade, or light shade
How deep to plant: Top of bulb neck just above soil surface
Hardiness: To about 25°F/−4°C; in colder regions, overwinter indoors

Gardeners might be tempted to grow *Veltheimia* just for its handsome foliage. Glossy, wavy-edged leaves, to 1 foot long and 3 inches wide, grow in a fountainlike rosette. At the tip of each brown-mottled flower stem is an elongated cluster of drooping tubular flowers in pale rose with green petal tips.

In frost-free regions, you can plant *Veltheimia* in the ground—but even so, most gardeners treat it as a container plant. *Veltheimia* can stay outdoors over winter only where winter temperatures remain above 25°F/−4°C; where frost is possible, give overhead protection.

Container culture. Plant the large bulbs in August or September; for each one, use a container large enough to allow about 3 inches between all sides of the bulb and the container edges.

Fill containers with the soil mixture described in directions "A" on page 91, then set in bulbs with the tops of their necks just above the soil surface. Place containers in a cool location and keep the soil just barely moist until growth begins. As growth continues, increase watering and provide more light and higher temperatures (around 60°F/16°C); apply a liquid fertilizer every 2 weeks throughout the growing season.

Reduce watering when foliage starts to die, and keep soil dry during summer. Resume regular watering when new growth appears in autumn. When containers become crowded with growth, dig and divide bulbs in late summer.

WATSONIA

Photo on page 75

Type of bulb: Corm
Season of bloom: Late spring, summer
Colors: Lavender, pink, salmon, rose red, reddish orange, white
Grows to: 3½ to 6 feet
When to plant: Late summer or early autumn; spring where winter temperatures fall below 10°F/−12°C
Where to plant: Sun
How deep to plant: 4 inches
Hardiness: To about 10°F/−12°C; in colder regions, dig and store deciduous types over winter as for *Gladiolus*

Watsonia elegantly combines stateliness and delicacy. The fans of swordlike foliage and upright spikes of double-ranked blossoms clearly reveal a close relationship to *Gladiolus*, but there are clear differences as well. *Watsonia*'s leaves are less rigid and its flower spikes taller and more slender; the fragrant blossoms are smaller and more trumpetlike.

Two *Watsonia* species (and hybrids of each) are commonly available. *W. beatricis* blooms in midsummer, sending up slightly branched 3½-foot-tall spikes from fans of 2½-foot evergreen leaves. The 3-inch-long blossoms are bright reddish apricot; you'll also find hybrids in colors ranging from peach to nearly red. *W. pyramidata*'s late spring blooms are borne on 4 to 6-foot spikes that rise above 2½-foot-long leaves; flower color is cool pink, rosy red, or white. Hybrid forms have pink, red, or lavender blooms. Foliage dies back after flowering, then reappears with the onset of cooler weather in late summer to early autumn.

Uses. *Watsonias* are handsome accent clumps in the background of mixed annual and perennial plantings, and even among shrubbery.

Garden culture. Choose a sunny location—preferably with well-drained soil, though *Watsonia* will perform in a great range of soils, from sandy to clay. Plant corms in early autumn, setting them 4 inches deep and 6 inches apart. Water regularly throughout the growing and blooming season; after blooming, cut back on water until autumn (plants in well-drained soil will accept regular summer watering).

Where corms are hardy in the ground, you can leave them undisturbed for a number of years. Dig and divide only when plant and flower quality decline. In regions where winter lows dip beneath 10°F/−12°C, evergreen *W. beatricis* cannot be grown successfully, since corms will not tolerate digging, drying, and subsequent replanting. However, you can grow deciduous *W. pyramidata* and its hybrids in these areas: dig corms when foliage dies back, store over winter as for *Gladiolus*, and replant when weather turns warm in spring.

ZANTEDESCHIA

CALLA
CALLA LILY

Photos on pages 13 and 75

Type of bulb: Rhizome
Season of bloom: Spring, summer
Colors: White, cream, yellow, pink, red, orange, buff, lavender, purple
Grows to: 1 to 4 feet
When to plant: Autumn, winter, or early spring
Where to plant: Sun, part shade, or light shade, depending on species and climate
How deep to plant: 2 to 4 inches, depending on type and climate
Hardiness: To about 10°F/−12°C; in colder regions, dig and store deciduous types over winter as for *Begonia*

The simple, streamlined beauty of white calla lilies is familiar to many from bouquets at ceremonial occasions. Admirers of Art Nouveau are also well acquainted with callas, since the blossoms were a popular motif in metal and glass pieces. Actually, the calla's "flower" is a cornucopia-shaped bract surrounding a central yellow spike (the spadix); the tiny true flowers cluster around the base of the spadix. All species have glossy, arrow-shaped leaves on erect stalks, but foliage color varies—the common calla's leaves are solid green, but other species often have variegated or spotted foliage.

The largest, most familiar species of *Zantedeschia* is *Z. aethiopica,* the common calla. Foliage clumps reach 2 to 4 feet, with individual leaves to 10 inches wide and 1½ feet long. Beginning in spring (sometimes continuing into summer), pure or creamy white 8-inch-long bracts appear on stems just slightly taller than the foliage. Variety 'Hercules' is larger than the species, with broad, recurving bracts that open out nearly flat. 'Green Goddess' has partially green bracts. Smaller varieties include 'Childsiana' (just 1 foot tall) and 'Minor' (1½ feet tall, with 4-inch bracts). For especially profuse bloom, choose 'Godefreyana'; it's only slightly smaller than the species.

Summer-blooming *Z. elliottiana* (golden calla) grows to 2 feet tall; its white-spotted bright green leaves reach 10 inches long and 6 inches wide. The 6-inch bracts are greenish yellow when they open, then change to a bright, rich golden yellow.

Z. albomaculata, the spotted calla, is about the same size as *Z. elliottiana* and has similar foliage. Its bracts differ, though—they're creamy yellow or white, with a red-purple blotch at the base. The blooming season extends from spring into summer.

Shortest of the species, growing only 1½ to 2 feet tall, is *Z. rehmannii*—the pink (or red) calla. Its foot-long leaves, typically unspotted, are lance shaped rather than arrow shaped. Four-inch pink to red bracts appear in midspring; 'Superba' is a dark pink selection.

Hybrid callas flower in late spring and summer. They're usually about the size of *Z. rehmannii;* bract colors include cream, buff, orange, pink, lavender, and purple.

Uses. An individual clump of any calla is sure to be an accent—in mixed groupings of other flowering plants, amid foliage plants, or surrounded by a ground cover. For an even showier effect, plant callas in drifts among lower growing plants.

Garden culture. Most callas need well-drained soil, liberally enriched with organic matter before planting. And all will thrive with regular watering the year around. Common calla appreciates additional moisture, even enjoying the soggy soil at the edge of a pond. Beyond these similar soil and water requirements, however, calla culture varies slightly depending on the species.

Common calla is basically evergreen, going only partly dormant even in the colder parts of its hardiness range. It cannot withstand storage, so it should be grown only as a container plant where winter temperatures fall below 10°F/–12°C.

In areas where temperatures remain above 20°F/–7°C, plant common calla rhizomes at any time from autumn through early spring, setting them 2 to 3 inches deep and a foot or more apart. In colder areas (down to 10°F/–12°C), plant in autumn or spring; cover rhizomes with 4 inches of soil. Common calla prefers part or light shade where summers are hot, but in cool or mild summer areas it will grow in sun, light shade, or part shade.

The other calla species and hybrids are deciduous: foliage dies down in autumn, then reappears in spring. Where winter temperatures remain above 10°F/–12°C, plant in autumn. In colder areas, plant in spring; then dig rhizomes each autumn after leaves wither and store over winter as for *Begonia*. Set rhizomes 2 inches deep, 8 to 12 inches apart. These callas will grow in full sun in any climate, though it's wise to provide part shade where summers are very hot.

Except in climates where annual digging is required, calla plantings may be left undisturbed for a number of years. Divide (at the best planting time for your area) only when overcrowding causes a decline in vigor and bloom quality.

Container culture. All callas are good container plants. For the deciduous kinds, follow directions "B" on page 91; common calla should be grown according to directions "C" on page 91.

ZEPHYRANTHES

FAIRY LILY
ZEPHYR FLOWER
Photo on page 75

Type of bulb: True bulb

Season of bloom: Primarily late summer

Colors: Pink, yellow, white

Grows to: 1 foot

When to plant: Early autumn; early spring where winter temperatures fall below 0°F/–18°C

Where to plant: Sun or part shade

How deep to plant: 1 to 2 inches

Hardiness: To about 10°F/–12°C; to about 0°F/–18°C with winter protection; in colder regions, dig and store over winter as for *Dahlia*

Zephyr flower's slender stems rise from clumps of grassy leaves; each bears a single funnel-shaped bloom. In mild climates, plants may bloom several times a year if you give them a short dry period after flowering, then resume regular watering to trigger a new growth cycle.

Z. candida is the most widely sold; its 2-inch blooms are white, sometimes stained with pink. *Z. citrina* is about the same size, but its fragrant flowers are lemon yellow. Rose pink *Z. grandiflora* bears 4-inch blossoms in late spring or early summer; leaves die back in autumn, then reappear at bloom time. Hybrids are available, with flowers in shades of pink and yellow.

Uses. See *Habranthus.*

Garden culture. Choose a planting site in sun or part shade; set out bulbs in well-drained soil, 1 to 2 inches deep and 3 inches apart. Water regularly from the time growth begins until bloom finishes. In frost-free regions, you can try for additional bloom cycles as described above; in colder regions, give little or no water after foliage dies back.

Where bulbs are hardy in the ground, you can leave them undisturbed for a number of years.

Container culture. Follow directions "C" on page 91.

THE FOUR SEASONS
OF BULB CARE

For many gardeners, a romance with bulbs begins under unromantic circumstances. Facing an array of nursery boxes or bins, the potential bulb grower is expected to believe that the drab objects they contain will somehow be transformed into the beautiful blossoms displayed in color photographs above each bin and box.

But after the first bloom season, when any lingering doubts have been erased by the actual garden appearance of those photographed images, subsequent bulb purchases will be made with confidence. Another gardener will have learned one of nature's truths: bulbs are easy to grow.

But though "easy to grow" is true, it does not confer a license for careless care. If you practice cavalier culture, you'll usually be "rewarded" by erratic performance at best. In the case of bulbs, "easy to grow" means that there are only a few strict requirements for success, and that those few needs are easy for gardeners to satisfy.

The first lesson to learn is that the following year's growth and bloom are determined by the current year's care. Bulbs selected from nursery bins or ordered from bulb specialists have been grown under optimum conditions to ensure a good display in your garden, given a little sensible attention. But if those bulbs are to stage an encore performance the next year, you must think about, and act on, their needs during that first dazzling bloom season.

The Catalog of Favorite Bulbs (pages 18 to 77) spells out the conditions in which each of the bulbs described will grow well. For greatest satisfaction, choose bulbs well suited to your particular climate—the summer and winter temperatures, the timing of rainfall. In the following pages, you'll learn the basics of bulb culture.

APPEARING yearly without fail, autumn nursery bulb displays are as predictable as spring and summer bloom.

BULB TYPES

To a botanist, the word "bulb" has a precise definition, referring only to true bulbs (as described below) and the plants that grow from them. Horticulturists and the general public, however, use "bulb" as a generic term for plants that grow from five distinct types of underground structures: true bulbs, corms, tubers, rhizomes, and tuberous roots. Certain aspects of basic culture differ from type to type, but one trait is common to all: function. These structures are storage organs, holding reserves of food that can keep the plant alive

THE FIVE BASIC BULB TYPES

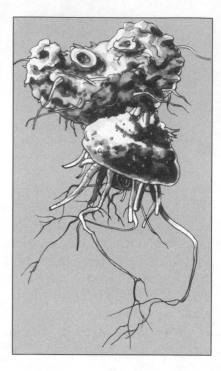

TRUE BULB

The true bulb is really an underground stem base with an embryonic plant—complete with leaves, stems, and flower buds—ready to grow when the conditions are right.

Surrounding this miniature plant are *scales:* modified leaves that overlap each other in a scalelike manner, giving the bulb as a whole a swollen, often pear-shaped appearance. The *basal plate,* at the bottom of the bulb, holds the scales together and produces roots.

Many bulbs—tulips and daffodils, for example—are sheathed in a papery skin called a *tunic,* which protects against both injury and dehydration. But other bulbs (such as lilies) lack this protective outer layer, so require more careful handling.

Individual bulbs may persist for many years, periodically producing *offsets* (new, smaller bulbs).

CORM

Gladiolus and crocus are two familiar favorites that grow from corms. Like a true bulb, a corm contains the base of a stem, but in this case the "bulb" tissue is solid—actually a swollen underground stem base—rather than a series of overlapping modified leaves. Roots grow from a basal plate at the corm's bottom. The principal growth point "sits" on top of the corm.

Some corms have tunics. These are often superficially similar to a bulb's tunic, but they're formed from the dried bases of the previous season's leaves rather than from a layer of modified leaves.

Each corm lasts just one year, depleting its stored energies in the growth and bloom process. But as it's shrinking away, a new corm forms on top of it; numerous offsets (called *cormels*) may also be produced around the new corm's base.

TUBER

Tubers, like corms, are swollen stem bases. But while a corm has a fairly clearly organized structure, a tuber does not. There is no tunic of any kind, nor is there a basal plate—roots grow from the tuber's base and sides, and sometimes from the top as well. And instead of just one or a few growing points, a tuber has multiple growth points scattered over its upper surface; each one is really a scalelike leaf with a growth bud in its axil.

An individual tuber can last for many years. Some (*Cyclamen,* for example) continually enlarge, but never produce offsets; others (such as *Caladium*) form protuberances that can be removed and planted separately.

(often in a dormant or semidormant condition) from one growing season to the next, through drought, cold, or other climatic adversities.

The characteristics of each of the five bulb types are summarized on these pages; in the box at right, plants described in the Catalog of Favorite Bulbs (pages 18 to 77) are listed by type. For information on how to divide bulbs, see pages 88 and 89.

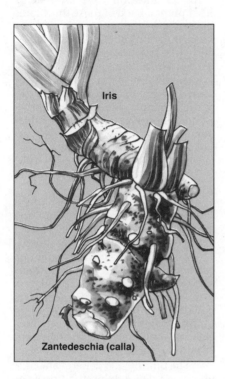

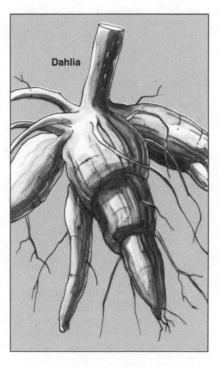

RHIZOME

Tall bearded irises are perhaps the best known rhizomatous plant, but a number of other popular "bulbs"—calla lilies and cannas, for examples—also grow from these structures. A rhizome is actually a thickened stem (with no basal plate) that grows horizontally, either partly or entirely underground. Roots grow from the rhizome's underside; the primary growing point is at its tip, encased in scalelike embryonic leaves. Additional growth points will form along the rhizome's top or sides.

Because growth proceeds horizontally and because additional growth points give rise to full-fledged new plants, a planting that began with an individual rhizome will grow larger each year, as more and more rhizomes reach out into surrounding soil.

TUBEROUS ROOTS

Of the five "bulb" types, only the tuberous root is a true root, thickened to store nutrients, rather than a specialized stem. In a full-grown dahlia, daylily, or other tuberous-rooted plant, the roots grow in a cluster, with the swollen tuberous portions radiating out from a central point. The growth buds lie on the roots' "necks", on bases of old stems, or as a "crown" where all roots come together. Normal fibrous roots, for water and nutrient intake, grow from the sides and tip of each tuberous structure.

Each tuberous root can give rise to an individual plant, as long as it's separated from the group with a growth bud attached to its neck (or to the old stem base just above it).

BULBS LISTED ACCORDING TO TYPE

TRUE BULB

Allium	Lachenalia
Amaryllis	Leucocoryne
Calochortus	Leucojum
Camassia	Lilium
Chionodoxa	Lycoris
Crinum	Muscari
Endymion	Narcissus
Eucharis	Nerine
Eucomis	Ornithogalum
Fritillaria	Oxalis (some)
Galanthus	Puschkinia
Galtonia	Scilla
Habranthus	Sprekelia
Haemanthus	Sternbergia
Hippeastrum	Tigridia
Hyacinthus	Tulipa
Hymenocallis	Vallota
Ipheion	Veltheimia
Iris (some)	Zephyranthes

CORM

Babiana	Gladiolus
Brodiaea	Ixia
Colchicum	Lapeirousia
Crocosmia	Sparaxis
Crocus	Tritonia
Erythronium	Watsonia
Freesia	

TUBER

Anemone (most)	Eranthis
Begonia	Gloriosa
Caladium	Oxalis (some)
Colocasia	Sinningia
Cyclamen	

RHIZOME

Achimenes	Dietes
Agapanthus	Iris (many)
Anemone (some)	Oxalis (some)
Belamcanda	Polianthes
Bletilla	Schizostylis
Bulbinella	Tulbaghia
Canna	Zantedeschia
Convallaria	

TUBEROUS ROOT

Alstroemeria	Eremurus
Clivia	Hemerocallis
Dahlia	Ranunculus

PURCHASE, PLANTING & CARE

Getting bulbs off to a good start is your best guarantee of success. In these six pages, we outline that good start from bulb purchase through soil preparation, planting, watering, and fertilizing.

Buying bulbs

Because a bulb's performance depends on the care the plant received in the previous season (see pages 88 and 89), your initial success depends on the grower and vendor of the bulbs you buy. For guaranteed good performance, purchase good quality stock: bulbs grown, stored, and shipped under ideal conditions.

A bulb's appearance and heft are the best clues to its general health. Choose firm bulbs; a soft, squashy feel usually indicates the presence of rot or tissue breakdown. In most cases, bulbs should also be plump and heavy for their size. Those that are light in weight or visibly shriveled may have lost too much moisture to perform well. (Two exceptions are anemone and ranunculus, which usually look unpromisingly shrunken.)

Bulb size does have a bearing on first-year performance. The largest tulip and hyacinth bulbs, for example, will produce larger flowers on thicker, taller stems than will the smaller sizes. In the case of ranunculus, large sizes will produce *more* flowers than smaller ones. But if you don't require the showiest possible blooms, or if you're willing to wait a year or two for bulbs to build themselves up in your garden, the smaller sizes are often an excellent buy.

Timing of bulb purchases is of great importance: most bulbs should be bought and planted in their state of greatest dormancy (exceptions are evergreen types such as *Clivia*, sold only as container-grown plants). For many plants—daffodils and tulips, for example—bulbs in the depths of dormancy are devoid of leaves and roots. In other cases (bearded irises, daylilies), the "bulb" will have live leaves and roots, but will be sold at an inactive period in its growth cycle.

In general, bulb sellers make bulbs available at their best planting times. But remember that retail nurseries and some mail-order firms may keep bulbs on the shelf for a period of time; those sold late in the season may have deteriorated. Always try to purchase and plant bulbs as soon as they're available. And always examine end-of-season sale bulbs carefully.

Nursery purchases

In retail nurseries and garden centers, early autumn usually brings out tempting displays of spring-flowering bulbs: a number of different kinds massed in boxes and bins, accompanied by alluring photographs of the blooming plants.

The retail nursery's greatest advantages are accessibility (you can buy on impulse) and the opportunity to see just what you're getting—both the condition of the bulbs and the shape and color of the flowers they'll produce.

The chief drawback is limited selection: the typical nursery or garden center finds it impractical to offer as large a selection as do some specialty mail-order suppliers.

BULB BUYING TIPS

You can't expect first-rate performance from second-rate stock. For greatest satisfaction:

Look for
- plump, firm bulbs
- bulbs available at proper planting time

Avoid buying
- shriveled or lightweight bulbs (with a few exceptions)
- soft or squashy bulbs
- bulbs obviously damaged in digging
- moldy bulbs or those with discolorations that aren't a part of the natural appearance

---

Bulbs by mail

Mail-order bulb catalogs separate into three categories: the ultra-specialist, offering only one or several kinds of bulbs; the general bulb specialist, selling a wide assortment; and the general nursery catalog, which lists certain popular bulbs in addition to a number of other plants. Each of these three falls short of the retail nursery in one respect: you don't see the actual bulbs until they arrive at your door.

The ultra-specialty bulb catalogs frequently cater to home gardeners whose special interest is the particular bulb sold, so offerings include expensive novelties in addition to less costly older varieties. Cost of individual bulbs is no real indication of quality; high price simply indicates newness and/or scarcity of stock.

In most cases, the ultra-specialty cataloger is also the grower and will dig and ship bulbs at the best possible planting time.

General bulb specialty catalogs can tempt you with a veritable supermarket of offerings. In contrast to ultra-specialists, general specialists usually do not grow their own bulbs. Instead, their stock is typically purchased from specialty growers and/or bulb brokers.

The quality of a general specialist's stock depends on the firm's selectivity in wholesalers and its insistence on quality. The best firms offer top-quality bulbs shipped at the right planting times—subject, however, to receipt of bulbs from suppliers. Freshness is comparable to that in good retail nurseries.

The greatest variation in quality is usually found in stock ordered from general nursery catalogs. Always check for stock guarantees and conditions under which money may be refunded if dissatisfaction or failure ensues. Also check stated shipping times for particular bulbs against the best planting times as noted on pages 18 to 77; avoid buying from firms that ship at less than ideal times.

A final precaution applies to all catalog orders: *beware of "tremendous bargain" sales*. Unscrupulous dealers may use such sales as outlets for poor quality stock.

Where to plant

The purchase of good-quality stock (see page 82) isn't the only prerequisite for success with bulbs. Planting location is also important; if you want good performance year after year, you must set out bulbs in areas that provide the conditions they need. The entries on pages 18 to 77 specify where to plant each bulb described.

Sun means full, bright sun; *filtered sun* is the dappled light that comes through a lattice or an open-branched tree. *Light* or *high shade* means as much light as possible without direct sun; *part shade* means sun for about half the day (preferably in the morning) and shade for the remainder. *Moderate shade* is the sort of light found in woodland conditions—the ground is shaded all day, but not darkly. Finally, *shade* refers to fairly deep shade, as under a solid tree canopy or against the north side of a wall.

At the same time you check sun/shade preferences, read about the bulb's water needs. If the bulb of your choice requires a dry summer, don't plant it alongside your summer-thirsty plants.

Improving the soil

In the entries on pages 18 to 77, directions often suggest that you "enrich" or "liberally amend" soil with organic matter. Simply defined, organic materials are the remains or byproducts of living organisms. For the gardener, these materials are usually decaying plant matter: peat moss, compost, sawdust, or animal manures.

These substances can benefit all soils, helping to provide a better environment for plant roots. Particles of organic matter lodge in the pore spaces between soil particles; in clay, they act as wedges to keep the soil particles from packing so closely, while in sand, they fill in between particles to retain moisture. A great number of organic materials are available. Peat moss and manures are sold nearly everywhere; compost is available to all gardeners willing to take time to prepare it.

SOIL TYPES

All soils are composed of mineral particles separated by minute air pockets called "pore spaces." When water enters soil, it fills these spaces; then, as gravity pulls it downward, air gradually refills the spaces. This water movement is called "drainage"; the speed at which it progresses—slow or fast—characterizes a soil as having poor or good drainage.

Most "bulbs" rot if kept saturated for any length of time. Thus, almost all require "well-drained soil"—soil that doesn't remain saturated for long after watering.

For the home gardener, soils can be generally described as *clay* (poorly drained, sticky or bricklike, hard to work) at one extreme, *sand* (well drained, dry, easy to dig) at the other.

The differences between clay and sand result from differences in the sizes and shapes of the particles making up each type of soil. Clay particles are minute and flattened; they stack closely together, like a pile of playing cards. Clay soils take in water slowly but retain it well—once wet, they can remain soggy, sticky, and poorly aerated for days.

Sand particles are much larger and more rounded than those of clay, fitting together about like a boxful of marbles; pore spaces are larger as well. Sand accepts water readily but doesn't hold it long, drying so quickly that lack of moisture can be a problem.

Because roots need both air and moisture, neither clay nor sand offers entirely congenial conditions. The compromise between the two is known as *loam;* it contains a mixture of different-sized soil particles plus organic matter (see "Improving the soil," at left), and offers both moisture retention and good drainage.

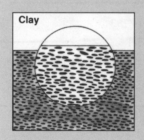
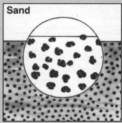
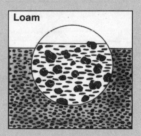

Many regionally produced byproducts of agriculture and industry are good soil amendments: redwood and fir bark from lumber-producing regions; sawdust; spent mushroom compost; ground corn cobs; apple or grape pomace (the residue from cider or wine making).

If you plan to amend your soil with manure or wood products (bark or sawdust), you'll need to take a few precautions. Fresh manures can actually harm roots—so if you use unaged manure, add it to the soil several months before planting. (If you dig in well-aged manure, you can plant right away.)

Wood products need nitrogen to assist their decomposition and will take from the soil whatever nitrogen they need. The result can be nitrogen-deprived plants. Packaged wood products are usually nitrogen-fortified, so they can be used directly. But if you use raw or untreated products, add 1 pound ammonium sulfate for each 1-inch-deep layer of organic material spread over 100 square feet. Scatter the ammonium sulfate over the spread-out organic matter, then dig it all into the soil. Wait about a month before planting.

One characteristic of all organic matter is that it is temporary: soil organisms are constantly at work breaking it down, so a finite quantity vanishes in time. Therefore, all soils will benefit from periodic additions of organic matter.

(Continued on next page)

Preparing the soil

Before planting bulbs, you'll need to loosen the soil and (usually) enrich it with organic matter (page 83) and fertilizer (pages 86 and 87).

Unless soil is already moist, water the planting area thoroughly.

When you can easily work the soil, dig the planting area to a depth of 9 to 12 inches. Break up any large soil lumps, then rake the soil surface flat.

Scatter fertilizer over the raked area; then spread on an even layer of organic matter. Use roughly 25 percent by volume of organic matter to soil; if you dig soil to a 12-inch depth, this works out to a 3-inch layer of organic material.

Finally, thoroughly incorporate the organic matter (and any other amendments) into the soil by hand digging or rotary tilling; then rake the soil even. If possible, let the prepared soil settle for at least a week before planting.

PLANTING DEPTHS FOR POPULAR BULBS

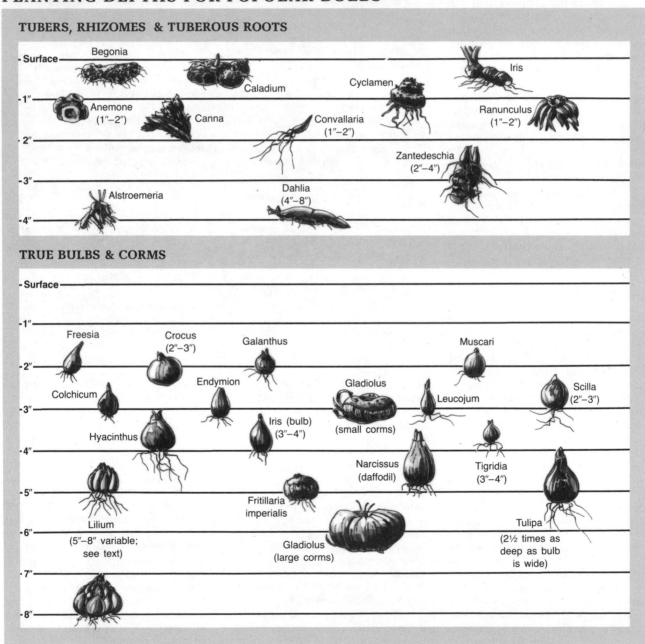

TUBERS, RHIZOMES & TUBEROUS ROOTS

Begonia · Caladium · Cyclamen · Iris
Anemone (1″–2″) · Canna · Convallaria (1″–2″) · Ranunculus (1″–2″)
Zantedeschia (2″–4″)
Alstroemeria · Dahlia (4″–8″)

TRUE BULBS & CORMS

Freesia · Crocus (2″–3″) · Galanthus · Muscari
Colchicum · Endymion · Gladiolus · Leucojum · Scilla (2″–3″)
Hyacinthus · Iris (bulb) (3″–4″) · Gladiolus (small corms)
Narcissus (daffodil) · Tigridia (3″–4″)
Fritillaria imperialis
Lilium (5″–8″ variable; see text) · Gladiolus (large corms) · Tulipa (2½ times as deep as bulb is wide)

Planting—the final step

If bulbs arrive at their correct planting times, you have only to check the proper planting depth and spacing before you plant. For each bulb described on pages 18 to 77, the preferred depth is noted under "How deep to plant"; appropriate spacing is mentioned in the text of each entry.

For a small number of bulbs, nothing has replaced the trowel as a handy planting aid. But if you have quite a few bulbs to set out, you may find that the bulb planting tool illustrated at right saves you both time and effort.

If you're planting a great number of bulbs of one kind in a formal arrangement, there's an even simpler method: excavate prepared soil to the proper depth, then set bulbs in place and fill in over them all at once. *Trenching* is a variation on this technique; you excavate strips of soil for planting bulbs in rows.

After planting, thoroughly water the soil to establish good contact between bulb and soil and to provide enough moisture to initiate root growth. After this initial watering, follow up according to the individual bulb's needs (see pages 18 to 77).

Foiling the spoilers

If your bulb plantings soon become gourmet gopher grub, and you've failed with (or have a distaste for)

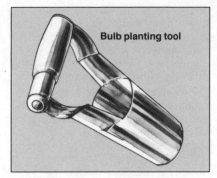

Bulb planting tool

BULB planting tool saves time and effort. A long-handled version is also sold.

traps or poisoned bait, try planting bulbs in wire baskets. The principle is exclusion—the mesh surrounding bulbs is tight enough to prevent gophers from getting to the bulbs inside, but loose enough for roots to penetrate freely into the soil.

It's simple to construct your own planting baskets from 1-inch (or finer) galvanized chicken wire. To make a basket for six to eight medium-size bulbs, cut a 12-inch-long section of 36-inch-wide wire. Twist or wire the ends together to form a 12-inch-high, 12-inch wide cylinder. To make the bottom, cut a 12-inch square of wire, then attach it to the cylinder's bottom by folding the corners up over the sides and hooking them into the mesh.

Once your baskets are ready, dig planting holes and slip the baskets into them. To discourage determined gophers from attacking bulbs from

above, position baskets so their rims extend at least 4 inches above the final soil level. Fill the baskets with soil to the proper depth for the bulbs you're planting; then plant bulbs.

You can use the same exclusion principle to make gopher-proof raised beds. After the bed is constructed (but before it's filled with soil), cover the bottom with chicken wire or $\frac{1}{2}$-inch mesh hardware cloth, letting the edges extend 2 to 3 inches up the sides of the bed. Then add soil and plant.

Watering

At least during the time when they're growing actively, bulbs need ample water. In their native habitats (see page 6), many of these plants have only a short time to flower and set seed before dry weather puts an end to the growing season. During this brief period, water must be plentiful enough to produce good initial bloom and to encourage vigorous growth, so bulbs can store a sizable reserve of nutrients for the next year's performance.

To do the greatest good, ample water must also be deep water. To cite an example: A daffodil bulb planted 6 inches deep will send its roots down for at least another 6 inches. If water is to benefit the roots, it must penetrate the soil far enough to reach them—in this case, to about 12 inches. A casual sprinkling obviously will not suffice.

(Continued on next page)

GIVE YOUR PLANTS THE RIGHT START

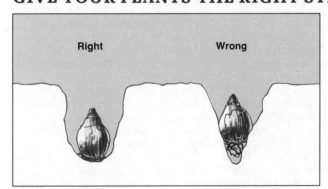

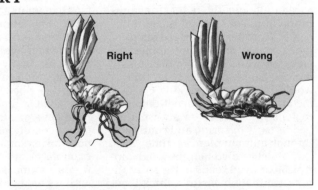

GOOD ROOT GROWTH depends on firm contact between bulb and soil. For bulbs that are rootless at planting time,

dig wide-based hole and set bulb securely on soil. For those with roots, make ridge of soil and spread roots downward.

In many regions, adequate deep moisture is usually supplied by rainfall in autumn, winter, and spring, or by snowmelt followed by spring rains. But you must help out when natural water is inadequate. As a general rule, *never let the root zone dry out during a bulb's growing season.* Water regularly enough to keep soil evenly moist, adjusting your watering to your soil type.

A month or so after flowers fade, the foliage of deciduous bulbs will yellow, signaling a shutdown in active growth and the onset of dormancy. At this point, you can cut back on water and let soil go dry (or nearly so), since most dormant deciduous bulbs need little or no moisture. (Some bulbs—*Ixia*, for example—have an absolute requirement for a dry dormant period.)

Evergreen bulbs' needs may differ from this general outline; consult the individual descriptions (pages 18 to 77) for water requirements.

One caution about watering: when bulbs are in flower, overhead watering can weigh down or topple stems. You may want to work out an irrigation system for use during the blooming period.

Mulches

Simply stated, a mulch is a layer of organic material on the soil surface. Nature supplies it in the form of fallen leaves and twigs; good gardeners realize its values and take pains to follow nature's lead.

Why mulch? A layer of organic material spread 2 to 3 inches deep over a planting greatly reduces evaporation of moisture from the soil beneath. Thus the soil surface remains moist longer and is not subject to cracking when dried by the sun. A mulch also keeps soil cooler than it would be if left bare. This cooling factor is of particular benefit in mild regions where warm to hot weather begins early in spring and continues through autumn planting time.

Mulches also help in weed control. Most weed seeds in the soil cannot germinate beneath a thick layer of organic material, and those that do sprout and grow are easy to pull because of the mulch's loose texture. In addition, there's an esthetic value to mulches: a uniform layer of organic material looks neat and tidy; it also prevents mud from splashing on foliage and low-growing flowers.

Last, but certainly not least, mulches improve the quality of the soil beneath. Organic matter gradually decomposes and becomes incorporated into the upper inches of the soil, improving its texture and ability to assimilate water.

Mulching materials. Any mulch must be sufficiently loose or coarse for water to penetrate easily. This rules out anything that compacts into an airless mass when moistened—thin-textured leaves or a thick layer of fresh grass clippings, for example. Beyond this restriction, though, your choices are quite varied. Wood and bark chips are widely used; thick-textured leaves (from evergreen oaks, for example) are also effective. Pine needles are popular wherever they're available. You can even use grass clippings if you spread them over the planting one thin layer at a time, allowing each layer to dry before adding another.

Some byproducts of regional agriculture also make excellent mulches—grape pomace (the residue from wine making) and rice hulls, for example.

Weed & pest control

Bulbs perform poorly if they fall victim to pests or diseases (see pages 94 and 95) or encounter stiff competition from weeds. As a bulb's most common adversary, weeds deserve elimination for reasons other than unsightliness. All weeds will compete for available moisture and nutrients; many will also compete for light and space. A number of the pests described on pages 94 and 95 find shelter among weeds, multiplying at a greater rate in these congenial conditions. The same conditions foster some diseases (rots, for example)—and what's more, the weeds may mask the disease activity until it's too late to cure the afflicted plants.

For weed control, nothing has superseded hand methods: pulling and, with care, hoeing. A mulch is a big help in preventing weed growth, and also makes it easier to remove those that do show up. Another effective prevention is the pre-emergent herbicide—but it must be used with extreme caution, following directions to the letter.

Fertilizers

Nearly all bulbs need fertilizer for best performance. In particular, they require the right type of fertilizer, applied at the right time.

Types of fertilizer. "Type" of fertilizer has two meanings. First, it refers to the physical form of a fertilizer: granular (dry), liquid, or timed-release. Granular fertilizer is the best choice for in-ground plantings, since it's easy to spread over large areas and incorporate evenly into soil. Liquid forms (fish emulsion, for example) and timed-release capsules are often preferred for container-grown plants (see page 90).

Fertilizer "type" also refers to the content of a fertilizer, in terms of its percentage by volume of nitrogen, phosphorus, and potassium. All three of these elements are important for good growth and bloom, but their specific functions differ (see box, facing page). Phosphorus and potassium are particularly important in the formation of healthy bulbs.

When to fertilize. The fertilizing schedule for bulbs differs slightly depending on whether you're setting out a new planting or caring for an established one. For new plantings, dig fertilizer into the ground when you plant; fertilize again after flowers fade. For established plantings, you may fertilize early in the growing season if you wish, but the one really critical time to fertilize is, again, just when the current flower crop has finished.

The best kind of fertilizer (in terms of nutrient content) to use at each time depends on the plant's needs at that part of its growth cycle and, to some extent, on the best method of applying each of the major nutrients. (See "How to apply fertilizer" and "A Fertilizer Primer," this page.)

During the growing season, only nitrogen will contribute to the appearance of that year's foliage and flowers. Applied as a bulb is growing in preparation for bloom, nitrogen can increase plant height, leaf size, and flower size. The fertilizers touted as "bulb foods" contain large amounts of phosphorus or potassium and little or no nitrogen; if applied early in the growing season, they'll have only a slight effect (or none at all) on the abundance and quality of that season's flowers. These fertilizers are most effective if applied later in the year.

After flowering ends, most bulbs continue growing for a time, assimilating nutrients that will provide energy for the next year's performance. The start of this stage—just after blossoms fade—is the one crucial time during a bulb's year for supplementary nutrient application. Some nitrogen can still be useful, but the greater need is for phosphorus. No-nitrogen "bloom foods" (0-10-10, for example) are best applied at this time; they'll help build up the bulbs for a good display of blossoms in the year to come.

The fertilizing schedule just outlined applies to spring and summer-flowering bulbs that enter a leafless dormant period a month or so after flowers fade. The same routine holds for bulbs that remain leafy during their summer dormant period—bearded irises, for example.

For autumn-flowering bulbs that grow during autumn, winter, and spring (*Amaryllis belladonna*, for example), use a different schedule. Fertilize once with a high-nitrogen fertilizer as foliage begins to grow, then perhaps again with a high-phosphorus type in spring before leaves start to yellow.

Some evergreen bulbs, especially those from tropical and subtropical regions, may need more than two applications of fertilizer during the growing season; they may also require fertilizer at other times of year. Instructions for these bulbs are given in the individual descriptions on pages 18 to 77.

How to apply fertilizer. Fertilizers that contain only nitrogen can be applied to the soil surface with the assurance that they will, in time, become available to the bulb's roots (nitrate types become available immediately; see box below). But the other two major elements must be applied near the root zone to do the greatest amount of good.

When you prepare soil for planting, dig in a complete high-phosphorus fertilizer or an incomplete high-phosphorus type such as superphosphate, following package directions for amounts. This will get the fertilizer into the potential root zone, where emerging roots can take advantage of it. If you're planting bulbs individually, dig a bit of fertilizer into the soil at the bottom of each hole, then cover it with 1 to 2 inches of soil.

For an annual post-bloom application to an established planting, you may be able to do no more than scatter the fertilizer over the soil surface and lightly scratch or dig it in, hoping that some of the phosphorus and potassium will reach deep enough to do a bit of good. If the bulbs are sufficiently far apart, though, you can do a more effective job. For a regularly spaced planting (rows, for example), dig narrow trenches close to bulb roots, about 8 inches deep; be careful not to damage roots. Scatter fertilizer in the trenches, refill them with soil, and water well.

For an irregularly spaced planting where trenching would be difficult, you can dig narrow 8-inch-deep holes, using a trowel or a bulb planting tool (see page 85). Place a small quantity of fertilizer in each hole, refill with soil, and water thoroughly.

A FERTILIZER PRIMER

Most commercial fertilizers are "complete," meaning that they contain the three major plant nutrients: nitrogen (N), phosphorus (P), and potassium (K). The percentage of each element is given as a number on the package label; for example, an 8-5-5 fertilizer contains by volume 8 percent N, 5 percent P, and 5 percent K. For best growth and bloom, a plant needs all three of these nutrients.

Nitrogen is the critical element, used to form proteins, chlorophyll, and the enzymes necessary for normal cell function and reproduction. If a plant receives too little nitrogen, leaves will turn yellow and growth will be stunted. An excess, on the other hand, produces rank, sappy growth that will be vulnerable to insects and disease.

Nitrogen is useful to plants only in its nitrate form; if applied in organic or ammonium form, the element must be converted to nitrate in the soil before roots can absorb it. But nitrates are water soluble, easily leached beyond the reach of roots. For this reason, plants require nitrogen in greater quantity than phosphorus or potassium, which "stay put" once they're applied.

Plants use *phosphorus* to form the nucleic acids important for early growth and for root and seed formation. This element is also significant in building healthy bulbs.

Unlike nitrogen, phosphorus is not water soluble. Instead, it binds chemically to mineral particles in the soil and is then taken up by roots. It must be applied where roots are (or where they are to be): dig it into soil or apply it in deep trenches. If you spread it on the soil surface, it will bind to particles in only the top inch or two of soil—and so will be assimilated by only the shallowest roots.

Potassium helps transport sugars and starches and is necessary for root growth, disease resistance, and fruiting. The water-soluble potassium in fertilizers goes through an intermediate step in the soil to become insoluble *exchangeable potassium,* which roots can absorb by contact. Potassium also should be applied at root level.

OFF-SEASON CARE

Your responsibility to your bulbs doesn't end when the last flower fades—or even when the last leaf withers. If you want to see good performance year after year, you must tend to each bulb's needs all year long, during dormancy as well as growth.

The importance of good care throughout the growing season becomes obvious if you keep in mind that a bulb is a storage organ. If it's to amass the greatest possible amount of food to fuel growth and bloom the next year, the plant must be kept green—and nutrient producing—until the present cycle ends. Even after bloom is over, you'll usually need to continue routine watering and fertilizing until active growth ceases, the plant matures, and you see indications that a dormant period is at hand.

Signals of dormancy vary, as does the timing, from bulb to bulb. Yellowing or withering foliage is one common indicator, but sometimes the signs may be more subtle; bearded irises, for example, simply appear to stop growing for a time, though their leaves don't fade.

Though dormancy is a period of inactivity, you shouldn't ignore your bulbs the moment you see that growth has stopped. Take care to give them proper winter protection if they need it; if you plan to dig and store bulbs, provide the appropriate conditions (see below). And if you need to divide your plantings, dormancy is usually the best time to do so.

Dividing

Most bulbs, in time, reward a gardener's care by forming increases ("offsets") that can be detached to establish new plantings. Some bulbs increase so slowly that you seldom need to dig and divide. But a great many others will proliferate with something approaching rabbitlike enthusiasm, compelling you to dig and divide periodically in order to relieve overcrowding and consequent reduced performance.

The illustrations below show the best method for dividing each "bulb" type.

Storage

The key to any bulb's need for storage is *climate:* many bulbs require protection from winter cold, while another, smaller group needs protection from summer moisture.

Every bulb has a hardiness limit—a temperature below which it cannot survive. The descriptions on pages 18 to 77 note each bulb's hardiness limit, and usually suggest means of storage in areas where winter weather is too cold for outdoor survival. Some bulbs, however, do not tolerate storage; for these, we state hardiness alone.

Bulbs requiring cold protection fall into two groups. Those in the first group are tender tropical and subtropical bulbs. Some go completely dormant (*Achimenes* and *Caladium,* for example) and may be stored in dark, dry conditions, still planted in their containers. But others are evergreen (*Clivia, Agapanthus*) and require light and water during their winter stay indoors.

The second group (sometimes referred to as "half-hardy") consists mainly of Mediterranean and subtropical bulbs that have a limited tolerance for subfreezing temperatures. Some can successfully winter outdoors in areas just a bit colder than their normal limits if given protection, but need storage where temperatures fall far below their hardiness limit.

A relatively small group of bulbs, typified by *Ranunculus* and *Calochortus,* must remain totally dry throughout their summer dormant period. Such bulbs are naturally most successful in regions where summers are dry, but even there they may be wanted for spring display in gardens that need summer watering. In this case, dig bulbs after leaves die back, store them over

HOW TO DIVIDE THE FIVE BULB TYPES

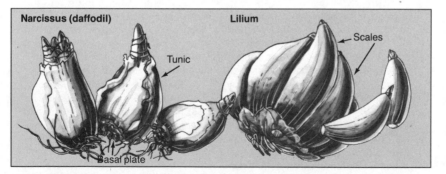

MANY TRUE BULBS (such as Narcissus) naturally separate into individual plants still connected to a common basal plate. To divide, carefully break apart connected bulbs at base. Lilies may increase in a similar manner, but you can also start new plants by carefully removing outer scales, dipping base ends in rooting hormone, and planting.

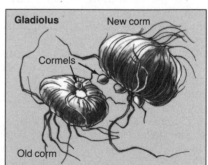

CORMS renew themselves each growing season by forming small increases (cormels). New corm and cormels form on top of old corm. To divide, separate new corm and cormels from old corm.

summer under controlled conditions, and replant at the normal time in late summer or autumn. Alternatively, you may grow some of these bulbs in containers, keeping soil dry over summer.

The hows & whys of storage

Two general methods cover the storage needs of all popular bulbs: *ventilated* and *covered* storage. Ideal storage temperatures vary a bit; check the descriptions on pages 18 to 77.

One general caution applies to all stored bulbs: they can become a veritable banquet for mice seeking winter shelter. If mice are likely to overwinter with your bulbs, securely cover or enclose them with hardware cloth or screening.

Ventilated storage. Bulbs that have a hard skin or a protective "tunic"—*Gladiolus* and *Ixia,* for example—can go through storage in mesh bags or piled loosely in boxes or baskets. Exposure to air keeps them dry, while the protective skin or sheathing helps prevent dehydration.

Preparation for storage differs slightly from bulb to bulb (check the entries on pages 18 to 77). In general, though, follow these steps:

When foliage has yellowed, dig bulbs from the ground or knock them from their containers. Remove leaves and soil; then spread out bulbs on newspapers in a shaded location and let them dry for 1 to 2 weeks. It's best not to separate bulbs before storage, since broken surfaces offer easy entry for disease organisms and heighten the chance of dehydration.

Store the dry, cleaned bulbs over winter; divide and replant the following year.

Covered storage. Dahlias, begonias, and a number of other bulbs lack a protective covering, so they'll begin to shrivel if left exposed to air for long after digging. If dehydration continues during storage, the bulb may die before replanting time.

Begin by digging and drying as directed for "Ventilated storage." Then place bulbs in a single layer in cardboard or wooden boxes or in clay pots and cover with sand, vermiculite, sawdust, perlite, or peat moss. You can store many bulbs in one container, but arrange them so their sides don't touch; should any bulb rot during storage, the separation lessens the chance of rot spreading from bulb to bulb.

Replant the next year, dividing bulbs then if necessary. If bulbs look dry or shriveled, plump them up in moist sand before planting.

Container-grown bulbs that require covered storage can be held over winter in their containers if the soil is kept completely dry. At replanting time, knock bulbs out of containers and repot in fresh potting soil mix for those that need yearly repotting.

Winter protection

The purpose of winter protection is twofold. First, it provides insulation against harsh cold: the soil temperature beneath the protection never drops as low as that of unprotected earth. The second purpose is temperature moderation, especially important in the snowless winter and in regions where alternating warm and cold spells are common. The protected ground remains colder during warm periods than unprotected ground, so plants under cover are kept inactive through any bursts of false springlike weather. Unprotected plants may respond to warm spells by starting to grow, only to be killed by following spells of freezing weather.

Preferred materials for winter protection vary depending on availability; regional favorites include salt or marsh hay, prairie hay, reed canary grass, ground corn cobs, and evergreen boughs. One important characteristic is common to all—they won't pack down airtight.

In autumn after the soil has frozen, spread a 4 to 6-inch layer of protective material over soil. Leave in place until just before the normal spring growing period begins.

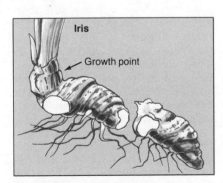

RHIZOMES produce new plants from growth points along their sides. To divide, break at the natural "waists" between sections, making sure each has at least one growing point.

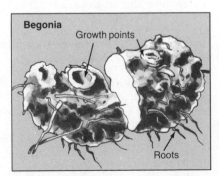

MANY TUBERS increase in size and number of growing points, but don't separate into more plants. To divide, cut large tuber into 2 or more sections— each with one or more growth points.

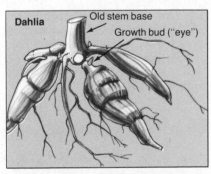

TUBEROUS-ROOTED PLANTS form multiple growth points, but not always separate plants. To divide, cut apart so that each separated root has a growth bud.

BULBS IN CONTAINERS

Growing bulbs in containers really entails no more effort than growing them in the ground. The few extra steps involved are balanced by reduced labor for soil preparation and planting. And since many bulbs will grow successfully in containers, you needn't worry about limited choices; the only real problem of choice is in narrowing the field.

By growing bulbs with successive flowering times, you can enjoy months of uninterrupted bloom: as one colorful potful of flowers fades, bring on another that's just coming into blossom. This "rotation" technique is particularly suitable for gardeners who want to grow many types of bulbs, but have little garden space.

Because containers are portable, a garden of potted bulbs can easily be rearranged to vary color groupings—or simply for a change of scene. In fact, the gardener who experiments with growing bulbs in containers often appreciates them more, since blooming plants can be positioned for close-up viewing.

Some bulbs are nearly always grown in containers—*Achimenes* and *Sinningia,* for example. Container requirements for these types are described in detail in the individual entries on pages 18 to 77. But many other bulbs commonly grown in the ground will also succeed in containers. On the facing page, these are grouped according to general cultural directions—"A," "B," or "C." (Any special container needs for particular bulbs are given in these plants' individual entries.)

For the techniques involved in forcing container-grown bulbs into early bloom, see pages 92 and 93.

Choosing a container

Clay (glazed or unglazed), plastic, and wood are the three most common container materials, but paper pulp pots and concrete and aggregate containers are gaining in popularity.

• Unglazed clay—the familiar red terra cotta pot available in many sizes and shapes—is the traditional choice. Plants in these containers require close attention to watering; moisture evaporates through the pot as well as from the soil surface.
• Glazed clay containers retain moisture better than unglazed ones, but they cost more and aren't sold in as many shapes and sizes. The glaze is often colored or patterned, so when you choose a pot, consider the possibility of color clash between the glaze and bulb's flowers.
• Plastic containers range from the purely utilitarian green or black nursery "can" to imitations of unglazed clay pots. They're as moisture retentive as glazed ceramic, though they're less attractive. But if looks aren't always in their favor, their low cost is.
• Wood containers offer a natural looking, neutral foil for plants of many types. You can buy containers ready made or build them to your own specifications. Wooden containers retain moisture as well as plastic and glazed ceramic; they're also better insulated (thanks to their thick sides), so soil is less likely to dry out rapidly in warm weather.

Whether you buy or build wooden containers, remember that decay-resistant wood—redwood, cedar, cypress—lasts the longest.
• Paper pulp pots are lightweight, inexpensive, and available in earthy colors of grayish tan to dark brown. Paper pulp is more moisture retentive than unglazed ceramic, but less so than plastic or wood. Its average life span is about 3 years.
• Concrete and aggregate containers are costlier and heavier than the previously mentioned types, but they're a lifetime investment. Design varies; some are absolutely plain, while others have a textured surface—"basketweave," rough and pebbly, or chiseled looking. Moisture retention equals that of plastic; insulation is the best of all types.

Whatever your choice in containers, make sure that all have drain holes. Containers that will hold the same bulbs for more than one year must offer enough room for root growth; 12 inches is a minimum depth, and deeper is better—especially for group "C" bulbs.

Watering

The individual descriptions on pages 18 to 77 indicate each bulb's water needs. The chief difference between in-ground and container culture is that container plants need to be watched more closely for dryness. Pay attention to the seasonal water needs of your container-grown bulbs, making sure to keep soil constantly moist when plants' moisture needs are greatest.

Fertilizing

For plants grown in the ground, one application of fertilizer a year is often sufficient. Likewise, bulbs to be grown in containers for just one bloom season will need no fertilizer beyond that incorporated into the potting soil (see directions "A" and "B" on the facing page). But bulbs that are to remain in containers for 2 years or more need extra attention.

The two most popular kinds of fertilizer for container plants are liquid and timed-release. Liquid fertilizers are concentrated nutrient solutions that you first dilute, then water into the soil. These fertilizers are available immediately to roots, but their solubility also has a drawback: nutrients are quickly leached from the container with subsequent waterings.

In general, liquid fertilizers should be applied once a month (if diluted according to label directions) or once every 2 weeks (if diluted to half the recommended strength). Always water soil thoroughly a day before applying the fertilizer solution.

Timed-release fertilizers are water-soluble dry fertilizers encased in small pellets with a permeable coating. You simply scatter pellets over the soil surface, then lightly scratch them in. This form of fertilizer provides nutrients over an extended period: each time you water, a bit of fertilizer dissolves and diffuses through the soil. For bulbs that die down after blooming, one application at the start of the growing season is sufficient; for evergreen types in group "C," a second dose may be required after about 4 months.

CONTAINER CULTURE

Not all container-grown bulbs need the same potting soil mix or the same care. Bulbs suitable for containers fall into three groups.

Group "A"

Bulbs in this group include *Achimenes, Begonia, Caladium, Gloriosa, Lachenalia, Oxalis, Polianthes, Sinningia,* and *Veltheimia.*

Specific container culture methods for *Achimenes, Begonia, Caladium,* and *Sinningia* are given in each plant's catalog entry. For the remainder, the following mixture is satisfactory:

    1 part peat moss
    1 part leaf mold or compost
    1 part perlite or builder's sand

When you fill pots, dig in superphosphate or a 5-10-5 fertilizer, following package directions for amounts.

For planting depth and spacing, check the individual bulbs' catalog entries.

Group "B"

Bulbs in this group fall into two categories.

The following bulbs perform well in a container for one season, but then should be planted in the garden: *Anemone coronaria, A. blanda,* and *A. fulgens, Crocus, Hyacinthus, Iris, Muscari, Narcissus, Puschkinia,* and *Tulipa.* Plant them in containers as shown in the illustrations below.

Other bulbs will succeed in containers for more than one year, provided that they receive their required dormant conditions. Bulbs in this category include *Alstroemeria, Babiana, Brodiaea, Calochortus, Colchicum, Convallaria, Cyclamen persicum, Endymion, Freesia, Ipheion, Ixia, Lapeirousia, Lilium, Ranunculus, Schizostylis, Sparaxis, Sternbergia, Tigridia, Tritonia,* and *Zantedeschia* (deciduous types).

Plant these bulbs a few inches apart, at the depths recommended in individual catalog descriptions. Divide and repot when flower quality and quantity decrease.

You can choose from two planting mixes for group "B" plants. For a fast-draining mix, use:

    1 part peat moss
    1 part other organic material
    (compost, leaf mold, nitrogen-stabilized bark)
    1 part builder's sand

If you prefer a slightly more moisture-retentive mixture using some good garden soil (not clay), try:

    1 part soil (loam to sandy loam)
    1 part peat moss
    1 part builder's sand

When you fill pots, mix in superphosphate or a 5-10-5 fertilizer, following package directions for amounts.

Group "C"

Bulbs in this category can remain in one container for several to many years. Many actually perform better when roots are crowded; they require repotting (and perhaps dividing) only when plants crowd the container almost to the bursting point.

Included in group "C" are *Agapanthus, Canna, Clivia, Colocasia, Crinum, Dietes catenulata, Eucharis, Eucomis, Habranthus, Haemanthus, Hemerocallis, Hippeastrum, Hymenocallis, Leucocoryne, Lycoris, Nerine, Ornithogalum arabicum* and *O. thyrsoides, Scilla peruviana, Sprekelia, Tulbaghia, Vallota, Zantedeschia aethiopica,* and *Zephyranthes.*

Plants in this group will do well in either of the soil mixtures recommended under method "B." When you fill containers, mix in superphosphate or a 5-10-5 fertilizer, following package directions for amounts.

Because these plants will remain potted for several years, be sure to choose containers deep enough to allow for root growth—at least 12 inches deep, preferably deeper. It's also best to plant in a container at least 8 inches across. Plant bulbs at the depths recommended in each plant's catalog description.

FOR BULBS in group "B" category I, follow this planting sequence: Set bulbs closely in potting soil; fill in, barely covering tops of bulbs.

PLACE CONTAINERS in cool location for 2 to 3 months while roots grow. Cover with sawdust or leaves to keep temperatures even.

UNCOVER when growth begins; keep in a filtered-light location until buds begin to show color, then move to desired display area.

FORCING

Because newly purchased bulbs already contain the embryonic bloom for the following season, you can—with a bit of extra effort—manipulate conditions to induce flowering before the bulb's normal outdoor blooming season. This process is popularly known as "forcing."

Forcing takes advantage of the fact that bulbs have certain minimum requirements for each stage prior to bloom. Because outdoor climate slows development, bulbs in the ground usually take more time than is minimally necessary in the prebloom stages. But under a forcing regime, you can control conditions so each stage is completed as quickly as possible.

For the most satisfying results, buy the largest top-quality bulbs you can find. Forcing draws heavily upon a bulb's food reserves, so those that have the greatest amount of stored energy will perform best.

Next, decide on the method of forcing you plan to use. Depending in part on the type of bulb, you can "plant" in water alone, pebbles and water, potting soil, or special "bulb fiber"; some bulbs require no rooting medium at all. Once you've chosen a method, calculate the best time to plant in order to achieve blossoms at the desired date. Most bulbs planted in potting soil will bloom 17 to 20 weeks after planting. On the other hand, narcissus grown in pebbles and water or in soil take just 6 weeks to flower.

With the exception of *Hippeastrum*, forced bulbs cannot be forced for a second season. After blooming is over, set bulbs out in the garden; in a year or two, they may build themselves up enough to flower at the normal time.

Recommended bulbs

Not all bulbs respond well to forcing, but those that do include the most popular of the spring-flowering types. Any of the following can be grown by the procedures outlined in the drawings below: crocus, hyacinth, *Iris reticulata* and related species, *Muscari* (grape hyacinth), narcissus, and tulip. You might also try freesia, Dutch iris, and *Scilla*; these three may need less time for root development.

Narcissus in pebbles & water

The autumn and winter-blooming *Narcissus tazetta* varieties do not need a prolonged cool, dark period for root growth before they send up leaves, so you can easily force them indoors in an entirely soilless medium. Most popular are the Chinese sacred lily (*N. tazetta* 'Orientalis') and the varieties 'Paper-white' and 'Grand Soleil d'Or'. The interval between starting and blooming is about 6 weeks. If you make your first

NESTLE Narcissus *bulbs into bed of small pebbles in 3 to 4-inch deep container. Keep water level at bulbs' bases.*

HOW TO FORCE BULBS

PLANT BULBS close together in either soil mix described in method "B," page 91; barely cover with mix. After potting, give a 12 to 16-week period at 40° to 45°F/4° to 7°C to allow roots to grow; cover pots with leaves or sawdust.

CHECK for top growth at 12 weeks; when growth starts, move to a well-lighted, fairly cool spot (55° to 60°F/13° to 16°C) for 2 to 3 weeks. When buds barely show color, move to a warm spot (72° to 75°F/22° to 24°C) receiving plenty of light.

planting in October, then plant at 2-week intervals until December, you can have flowering *Narcissus* indoors over a 2-month period.

Hyacinth and crocus in special glass containers

Both hyacinths and crocuses can be grown in water alone if you use the special glass vessels made just for this purpose. These containers look something like exaggerated egg cups: the bulb rests securely in the smaller upper section, while roots grow into the larger, water-filled lower part.

To "plant" the glasses, fill them with just enough water to touch the bulb's base, then add a small piece of activated charcoal to help prevent the growth of algae. Place the planted glasses in a dark, cool place (around 55°F/13°C) until roots are well developed and top growth has begun; add more water as necessary during this time to keep the level just beneath the bulb's base. When growth is underway, transfer glasses to a room with plenty of light and relatively cool temperatures (65° to 68°F/18° to 20°C). You can expect blossoms in 3½ to 4 months.

Amaryllis (*Hippeastrum*) for winter bloom

With a minimum of effort, you can bring amaryllis (*Hippeastrum*) into bloom for the winter holidays. All it takes is water, light, and about 6 weeks' time. Nurseries and mail-order firms offer bulbs already planted in special plastic containers; if you buy one of these, all you have to do is water and wait. Or buy bulbs and pot them up yourself, using either soil mix noted in directions "B" on page 91.

Nurseries usually offer one or more types of amaryllis bulbs: African, Dutch, Giant Dutch, Royal Dutch, or Ludwig Hybrids. For winter holiday bloom, choose those labeled African. These are grown to blooming size in South Africa, then stored and shipped under controlled conditions. When removed from cold storage, the bulbs sprout quickly and flower in 4 to 6 weeks. For sure bloom at Christmas, plant bulbs around November 15.

Most Dutch and Ludwig varieties are dug and shipped from Holland in September. These will bloom 7 to 8 weeks after planting.

If you want to *delay* the flowering of any of these amaryllis until later in winter or even until spring, wrap the bulbs in newspaper and store them in the refrigerator vegetable crisper at a temperature of around 40°F/4°C. Four to 8 weeks before the target flowering date (depending on the source of bulbs), remove bulbs and plant them in containers.

For each bulb, choose a container that allows 2 inches between the bulb and the container sides. Fill containers with one of the soil mixes recommended in "B" (page 91); plant each bulb so its neck and top half protrude above soil surface.

Water thoroughly after planting; then give just enough water to keep soil barely moist, but not soggy, until active growth begins. Keep containers in a bright, warm room (60° to 65°F/16° to 18°C at night, 70° to 75°F/21° to 24°C during the day); turn containers frequently so flower stems will grow upright rather than leaning toward the light source.

Once flowers open, you can lengthen their life if you move plants to a cooler location. As each bloom fades, cut it off to prevent seed formation. After all flowers have withered, cut off the entire stem at its base.

Leaves appear either during or after bloom, then die back when weather cools in autumn. For good performance the following year, it's important to keep the plant growing vigorously until foliage withers naturally—water regularly and give bimonthly applications of liquid fertilizer diluted to half strength. When the weather warms, you can move plants outdoors to a spot in filtered sun, part shade, or light shade.

When foliage yellows, cut it off; then store potted bulbs in a cool closet, basement, or garage where temperatures will remain above freezing (ideally around 40° to 50°F/4 to 10°C). If leaves haven't yellowed by autumn, withhold water in October to force dormancy, then store as directed.

In late December or during January, move the potted bulbs back into a bright, warm room and resume watering to start the next growth and bloom cycle.

Bulbs potted in "bulb mix"

Certain spring-flowering bulbs can be forced in "bulb mix" or "bulb fiber." For this variation on the standard technique (see facing page), you use a drainless container and a fibrous planting medium that holds moisture without becoming soggy. Because drainage is not necessary, you can use any watertight container —bowl, casserole, mug, vase, vegetable dish—and you can display the blooming bulbs on any surface, without having to place a drip saucer beneath.

The best bulbs for this method are those with short-stemmed blossoms; if you want to use taller types, make sure they're small flowered as well. Good choices are crocus; hyacinth; varieties and hybrids of *Tulipa greigii* and *T. clusiana*; *Iris reticulata*; *Muscari*; and smaller flowered *Narcissus*.

You can purchase bulb fiber from a nursery or make it yourself. The standard mix contains six parts by bulk of finely shredded sphagnum peat moss, soaked and then lightly squeezed to remove excess moisture; two parts crushed oyster shell; and one part crushed charcoal. Mix all ingredients well before filling containers. If you wish, use a simpler medium of peat moss alone (soaked and squeezed); if you do, place a thin layer of charcoal on the bottom of each container to keep the planting mix sweet.

Plant and cool-treat bulbs as directed in the sequential illustrations on the facing page, but be sure to place a sheet of plastic or other waterproof material over the pots before you cover or bury them. This will prevent rain from soaking through and drowning the bulbs in their drainless containers.

When you bring pots inside, keep them in a bright, cool room while foliage and stems grow. When buds show color and begin to open, you can transfer pots to another room for display. While plants are indoors, water the bulb mix carefully to keep it damp but not wet.

PESTS & DISEASES

Fortunately, bulbs as a group are potentially bothered by a fairly small number of pest and disease problems. By purchasing only healthy, top-quality bulbs, you can minimize the chances of encountering serious trouble.

Nonetheless, there are a few pests and diseases that are common enough to need special mention.

Aphids

Soft, rounded, and up to matchhead size, aphids may be green, pink to reddish brown, or black. They cluster on new growth, sucking plant juices; heavy infestations can devitalize a plant, distort growth, and aid in the spread of viruses (see next page).

Afflicted plants often also suffer from sooty mold, since the pests secrete a shiny "honeydew" that encourages mold growth on leaves. Sooty mold interferes with normal leaf functions, eroding a plant's health.

Controls: Aphids are easy to dispatch. Wash them off with water from a hose or with insecticidal soap (not detergent) and water. Or spray plants with pyrethrins, rotenone, diazinon, or malathion.

Thrips

These are tan, brown, or black insects, so tiny as to be barely visible. They feed on petals, causing distortion and discoloration; white and pastel colored blooms are particular favorites. In severe infestations, buds become so distorted that they cannot open. Thrips also attack foliage, causing distortion and silver gray to brown streaks.

To test for the presence of thrips, tap a blossom over a piece of white paper and watch for the appearance of tiny, moving specks.

Controls: Spray with malathion, metasystox-R, or orthene. Repeat in 10 to 14 days to kill any thrips that may have hatched after the first spraying.

Mites

Various mites can inflict damage in two ways: to flowers and to leaves of growing plants (usually during summer), and to bulbs in storage. The pests are almost invisible without a magnifying glass, but a sure sign of their presence is mottling on leaf surfaces and webbing on leaf underside. Infected bulbs are soft.

Mites reproduce very rapidly, so heavy infestations can develop quickly. If the infestation accompanies bulbs into winter storage, mites will enter bulbs through injured or damaged areas, stunting the next year's growth or even killing the bulb.

Controls: Spray growing plants with kelthane or orthene. When you dig bulbs, destroy the cut-off tops; then dust bulbs with diazinon before you store them. Before planting, examine bulbs carefully and destroy any that feel soft.

Mealybugs

Bulbs grown as house plants, in containers, or in areas where air circulation is poor are most susceptible to mealybug infestation. These rounded to oval insects are white and fuzzy looking; though large enough to be seen (about $\frac{1}{8}$ inch across), they're usually hidden at the bases of stems or leaves. Like aphids, they're sucking insects that devitalize the infested plant, distort foliage, and assist the spread of viruses. They, too, secrete a honeydew that offers a foothold for sooty mold.

Controls: Spray infested plants with diazinon, malathion, or orthene (add a spreader-sticker to the solution to enhance contact).

Iris borer

This iris borer is a potential problem only in the area from Iowa to the Atlantic Ocean, southern Canada to Tennessee. This moth larva attacks rhizomatous irises, eating both foliage and rhizomes.

Overwintering eggs hatch in early spring; during May and June, the brown-headed, white larvae grow from $\frac{1}{8}$ to about $1\frac{1}{2}$ inches long, eating their way down the leaves and finally entering the rhizomes. Larvae make pinholes and ragged edges on leaves; they hollow out rhizomes and, if infesting established clumps, will travel to connected rhizomes. The drab brown adult moths appear from mid-September to late October, laying clusters of eggs largely in the dry debris around plants.

Controls: Thorough autumn garden cleanup will remove many eggs. Hand pick and destroy any borers you see on foliage in spring and summer. From the time leaves are 6 inches long until the end of June, spray weekly with malathion or cygon.

Narcissus bulb fly

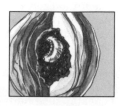

The narcissus bulb fly's larvae damage or destroy bulbs of *Narcissus,* and also attack closely related bulbs such as *Galanthus, Leucojum,* and *Hymenocallis.* Adult flies look like two-winged bees; in spring, they lay eggs at the bases of stems and leaves. Eggs hatch into grubs that either eat down into the bulb or burrow into the soil and attack bulbs at their basal plates. Grubs feed on bulbs from spring until early autumn, then overwinter inside the bulbs. Infected bulbs are soft and squashy, each containing a plump $\frac{3}{4}$-inch grub.

Controls: Examine bulbs carefully at planting time and discard any that are infected (squash the grubs first). If you've had previous infestations, dust foliage and surrounding soil with diazinon after leaves emerge in early spring.

Slugs & snails

Slowing moving, night feeding molluscs will voraciously feed on leaves, stems, and even flowers of many plants, leaving telltale trails of silvery slime in their wake. They live in damp, cool, shady places—among garden litter or in woodpiles, for example.

Controls: Hand picking and various forms of lethal dispatch are traditional.

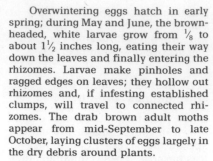

Search out and squash slugs and snails on damp, gray days, or hunt them down at night with a flashlight. Dry metaldehyde bait (toxic to dogs and cats when fresh) and mesurol bait (toxic to earthworms and insects) are effective. Slugs are attracted to saucers of beer; set out the "bait" at night, then collect and discard the victims the next morning.

Rodents

Many bulbs are gourmet treats for chipmunks, gophers, mice, squirrels, and ground squirrels. Gophers do their work entirely underground; mice may also do some tunneling to get at bulbs, but they're more likely to damage bulbs in storage over the winter. Chipmunks and ground squirrels will dig up recently planted bulbs, but don't usually bother established or stored ones.

Controls: Casual gopher infestations can be dealt with by setting traps or placing poisoned bait in gopher runs. Persistent problems, however, are better handled by planting bulbs in wire baskets or wire-bottomed raised beds (see page 85) or in containers.

To protect stored bulbs from mice, cover all bulbs with mouse-proof ¼-inch wire mesh (or place them in wire mesh containers). Thwart ground squirrels and chipmunks by placing chicken wire securely over new bulb plantings.

Botrytis

A number of foliage and flower blights are caused by various *Botrytis* species. A single infested bulb can spread the disease to an entire planting; epidemics also result from setting out bulbs in soil where the fungus exists on remains of infected plants.

Botrytis spores germinate and infect new leaves as new growth elongates, primarily in the moist weather of early spring. If damp conditions continue, powdery masses of spores form and are blown by the wind onto other plants. Brown- or gray-spotted leaves and fuzzy mold spreading over unhealthy, decaying leaf tissue are sure signs of *Botrytis* infection.

Controls: Remove and destroy diseased plants to eliminate sources of infection. Spray plants and surrounding soil with benomyl. If you're planting where infection has previously been present, spray with benomyl as foliage emerges in spring. If you dig bulbs from an infected area, soak them for 30 minutes in a benomyl solution (2 tablespoons benomyl to 1 gallon of tepid water) before storing.

Bulb rots

Several organisms can cause the slimy tissue breakdown referred to as rot. Rots may occur during warm or cool weather, but they're always associated with—and fostered by—moist or wet soil.

Fusarium basal rot afflicts true bulbs; it's encouraged by moisture and temperatures above 70°F/21°C. If a bulb contracts the disease while in the ground, foliage will yellow and rot while the bulb decays. Stored bulbs will become soft; they'll also spread the disease to any other stored bulbs touching them.

Crown rot, caused by *Sclerotium rolfsii,* also flourishes in moist soil during hot weather. Leaves rot off at their bases, which usually show some white webbing dotted with yellowish to black, pelletlike structures about the size of mustard seeds. These pellets are the fungus's "resting bodies" (*sclerotia*), which enable it to survive from year to year.

Some rhizomatous plants, notably bearded irises, develop soft rot on rhizomes or where leaves and rhizomes join. This rot often enters the plant via insect or mechanical injury, developing into a foul-smelling patch that can be fatal.

Controls: Rots are among the most difficult of diseases to control. They're usually discovered after the damage is beyond repair, and often persist in the soil once they've been introduced.

The best control for rots is to plant bulbs in well-drained soil. Since all rots thrive in wet soil, you can often avoid trouble—and virtually eliminate soft rots—by providing good drainage (see page 83). Beyond this basic measure, though, there are a few other steps you can take to eradicate rot problems.

For all but crown rot and soft rot, soak all sound bulbs taken from infected soil in the benomyl solution recommended as a treatment for *Botrytis* (at left); replant in fresh soil.

Crown rot can be controlled with fungicides containing PCNB. Badly in-fected plants must be destroyed, but you can save lightly infected ones by cutting out and destroying all rotted tissue. Soak soil and all salvaged plants with a PCNB solution mixed according to package directions. If you continue to grow the same type of plant in previously infected soil, you'll have to repeat fungicide drenches periodically.

For soft rot, scrape away rotted tissue; replant when wounded areas have dried.

Viruses

Viruses are microscopic organisms that live within a plant's tissues, usually causing some reduced vigor and flower distortion. Streaking on petals is a typical sign of infection; the streaks may be colorless—almost watery—or in a contrasting color (often bluish). Foliage may also show streaking, often in pale green or yellow.

Gladiolus, bulbous irises, and lilies are particularly prone to virus problems. In one case, the infection is decorative: "broken" tulips get their striped, variegated patterning from virus infection.

Controls: To prevent spread of viruses, remove infected plants from your garden (or isolate "broken" tulips from plantings of regular kinds). Also be sure to control sucking insects such as aphids, which can transmit the infection.

Powdery mildew

This fungus disease shows as a white or gray, powdery or mealy coating on the leaves, stems, and flower buds. Severe infestations debilitate a plant, robbing its tissues of nutrients and causing early death of leaves. Once the disease gets started, it will spread to other susceptible plants by windblown spores.

Powdery mildew develops in humid conditions, particularly in shade and where air circulation is poor. It also exists in arid regions where warm, dry days are followed by cool, moist nights.

Controls: Avoid planting in shady spots where air circulation is poor. Spray infected plants with benomyl, folpet, or cyclohexamide.

INDEX

Boldface numerals refer to main entry in
"Catalog of favorite bulbs"